Detroit Tigers 2019

A Baseball Companion

Edited by Patrick Dubuque, Aaron Gleeman and Bret Sayre

Baseball Prospectus

Craig Brown and Dave Pease, Consultant Editors
Rob McQuown and Harry Pavlidis, Statistics Editors

Library of Congress Cataloging-in-Publication Data:
paperback
ISBN-13: 978-1-949332-08-7

Project Credits
Cover Design: Kathleen Dyson
Interior Design and Production: Jeff Pease, Dave Pease
Layout: Jeff Pease, Dave Pease

Baseball icon courtesy of Uberux, from https://www.shareicon.net/author/uberux

Ballpark diagram courtesy of Lou Spirito/THIRTY81 Project, https://thirty81project.com/

Manufactured in the United States of America
10 9 8 7 6 5 4 3 2 1

Table of Contents

Foreword v
  Rob Mains

Statistical Introduction vii

Part 1: Team Analysis

Table for Two: Previewing the 2019 Detroit Tigers 3
  Patrick Dubuque and Matt Sussman

Performance Graphs 7

2018 Team Performance 8

2019 Team Projections 9

Team Personnel 10

Comerica Park Stats 11

Tigers Team Analysis 13

Part 2: Player Analysis

Tigers Player Analysis 20

Tigers Prospects 99

Part 3: Featured Articles

The Hole in The Shift is Fixing Itself 113
  Russell Carleton

The State of the Quality Start 117
  Rob Mains

Heads-Up Hacking—The First Pitch 123
  Matthew Trueblood

A Hymn for the Index Stat 129
  Patrick Dubuque

Index of Names 133

Foreword

Rob Mains

Welcome to this companion of the 2019 Detroit Tigers. We at Baseball Prospectus are excited to provide this analysis of the Tigers.

Our website, Baseball Prospectus, is a leader in delivering high-quality commentary and data to baseball fans everywhere. To some, those words—commentary and data—appear mutually exclusive. There are people out there who believe that traditional analysis and advanced analytics must run on different paths. But the simplistic narrative of stats vs. traditionalists just isn't true. Every team's analytics department interacts with scouting, development, and major league operations with a common goal: Delivering a championship. New technologies, like radar tracking of pitch speeds and movement, enable talent evaluators to focus on qualitative aspects of pitching like mechanics and pitch sequencing. In-game strategies like infield shifts, based on batters' hit tendencies, help turn balls in play into outs. Hitters use information to adjust their swings to maximize run production.

All these numbers can seem, at best, intimidating, and at worst, counterproductive to the casual fan. Even as technology and analysis have embedded themselves deeply into the way teams run, it can often feel like statistics create a displacement between the viewer and the sport, breaking them out of the action. And yet every fan incorporates the numbers to some degree; stats like batting average and earned run average, so fundamental to how we talk about performance, are actually complicated formulas. They don't bother people because those formulas have become second nature, as easy to translate as the action on the field.

Along the way, new statistics have entered baseball's lexicon. You'll see some of them, like on-base percentage (which measures a batter's ability to get on base via walk, hit batter, or hit), OPS (on-base plus slugging), and average exit velocity (the speed of balls off a hitter's bat) on broadcasts. Others, like DRC+, might well be new to you. Some of them have been well-defined to the public, others haven't. That lack of context has created ambiguity. Fans know that a ball hit 100 mph is scorched, but does that mean extra bases? (Not if it's hit on the ground or high in the air it doesn't.)

For those who are amenable to them, the new statistics can increase the enjoyment and understanding of the game. They can help fans identify when a pitcher is tiring, when a stolen base or a bunt attempt makes sense (and, more often, when it doesn't), or how a team's lineup might be constructed. Websites like Baseball Prospectus add to that understanding by weaving metrics into the narrative of the game. That's the goal of this publication: to take some of the newer, more complicated statistics and make them as intuitive as the ones on the back of old baseball cards.

But you don't need to love analytics to love baseball. The fans at BP who worked together to write this guide are captivated first and foremost by the game itself. We're drawn to Aaron Judge's power, Francisco Lindor's glove, Billy Hamilton's speed and Patrick Corbin's slider and don't need numbers to tell us why they're so mesmerizing. The underlying statistics provide depth to the game that we all love.

We hope you'll find that this guide helps you better understand the Tigers. Our analysts have studied the team's major league personnel and its minor league affiliates to identify their strengths and weaknesses, both the obvious ones and those that only a careful dissection of players' performances—yes, including the data—can reveal. You don't need us to tell you who was good and who wasn't in 2018, but our models and writers can help you project how each player is going to perform this year and beyond, and appreciate the greatness of each new game as it unfolds. As in the sport itself, the human and analytic components combine to generate a deeper overall understanding.

Think back to the first time you saw a baseball game on a high-definition TV. You'd grown familiar with how the game looked and felt on a picture tube. But new TV allowed you to see details that you'd never seen before. That's how advanced statistics work. The game itself is why you're here and why you're buying this. (And, for that matter, why we wrote it.) The statistical measures provide the sharper focus, the detail, the depth of knowledge that you didn't have before, generating an overall superior picture. Enjoy the view.

—Rob Mains is an author of Baseball Prospectus.

Statistical Introduction

Sports are, fundamentally, a blend of athletic endeavor and storytelling. Baseball, like any other sport, tells its stories in so many ways: in the arc of a game from the stands or a season from the box scores, in photos, or even in numbers. At Baseball Prospectus, we understand that statistics don't replace observation or any of baseball's stories, but complement everything else that makes the game so much fun.

What stats help us with is with patterns and precision, variance and value. This book can help you learn things you may not see from watching a game or hundred, whether it's the path of a career over time or the breadth of the entire MLB. We'd also never ask you to choose between our numbers and the experience of viewing a game from the cheap seats or the comfort of your home; our publication combines running the numbers with observations and wisdom from some of the brightest minds we can find. But if you *do* want to learn more about the numbers beyond what's on the backs of player jerseys, let us help explain.

Offense

At the end of this past year, we've revised our methodology for determining batting value. Long-time readers of Baseball Prospectus will notice that we've retired True Average in favor of a new metric: Deserved Runs Created Plus (DRC+). Developed by Jonathan Judge and our stats team, this statistic measures everything a player does at the plate–reaching base, hitting for power, making outs, and moving runners over–and puts it on a scale where 100 equals league-average performance. A DRC+ of 150 is terrific, a DRC+ of 100 is average, and a DRC+ of 75 means you better be an excellent defender.

DRC+ also does a better job than any of our previous metrics in taking contextual factors into account. The model adjusts for how the park affects performance, but also for things like the talent of the opposing pitcher, value of different types of batted-ball events, league, temperature, and other factors. It's able to describe a player's expected offensive contribution than any other statistic we've found over the years, and also does a better job of predicting future performance as well.

The other aspect of run-scoring is baserunning, which we quantify using Baserunning Runs. BRR not only records the value of stolen bases (or getting caught in the act), but also accounts for a runner's ability to go first to third on a single or advance on a fly ball.

Defense

Where offensive value is *relatively* easy to identify and understand, defensive value is ... not. Over the past dozen years, the sabermetric community has focused mostly on stats based on zone data: a real-live human person records the type of batted ball and estimated landing location, and models are created that give expected outs. From there, you can compare fielders' actual outs to those expected ones. Simple, right?

Unfortunately, zone data has two major issues. First, zone data is recorded by commercial data providers who keep the raw data private unless you pay for it. (All the statistics we build in this book and on our website use public data as inputs.) That hurts our ability to test assumptions or duplicate results. Second, over the years it has become apparent that there's quite a bit of "noise" in zone-based fielding analysis. Sometimes the conclusions drawn from zone data don't hold up to scrutiny, and sometimes the different data provided by different providers don't look anything alike, giving wildly different results. Sometimes the hard-working professional stringers or scorers might unknowingly inflict unconscious bias into the mix: for example good fielders will often be credited with more expected outs despite the data, and ballparks with high press boxes tend to score more line drives than ones with a lower press box.

Enter our Fielding Runs Above Average (FRAA). For most positions, FRAA is built from play-by-play data, which allows us to avoid the subjectivity found in many other fielding metrics. The idea is this: count how many fielding plays are made by a given player and compare that to expected plays for an average fielder at their position (based on pitcher ground-ball tendencies and batter handedness). Then we adjust for park and base-out situations.

When it comes to catchers, our methodology is a little different thanks to the laundry list of responsibilities they're tasked with beyond just, well, catching and throwing the ball. By now you've probably heard about "framing" or the art of making umpires more likely to call balls outside the strike zone for strikes. To put this into one tidy number, we incorporate pitch tracking data (for the years it exists) and adjust for important factors like pitcher, umpire, batter, and home-field advantage using a mixed-model approach. This grants us a number for how many strikes the catcher is personally adding to (or subtracting from) his pitchers' performance ... which we then convert to runs added or lost using linear weights.

Framing is one of the biggest parts of determining catcher value, but we also take into account blocking balls from going past, whether a scorer deems it a passed ball or a wild pitch. We use a similar approach–one that really benefits from the pitch tracking data that tells us what ends up in the dirt and what doesn't. We also include a catcher's ability to prevent stolen bases and how well they field balls in play, and *finally* we come up with our FRAA for catchers.

Pitching

Both pitching and fielding make up the half of baseball that isn't run scoring: run prevention. Separating pitching from fielding is a tough task, and most recent pitching analysis has branched off from Voros McCracken's famous (and controversial) statement, "There is little if any difference among major-league pitchers in their ability to prevent hits on balls hit in the field of play." The research of the analytic community has validated this to some extent, and there are a host of "defense-independent" pitching measures that have been developed to try and extricate the effect of the defense behind a hurler from the pitcher's work.

Our solution to this quandry is Deserved Run Average (DRA), our core pitching metric. DRA looks like earned run average (ERA), the tried-and-true pitching stat you've seen on every baseball broadcast or box score from the past century, but it's very different. To start, DRA takes an event-by-event look at what the pitchers does, and adjusts the value of that event based on different environmental factors like park, batter, catcher, umpire, base-out situation, run differential, inning, defense, home field advantage, pitcher role, and temperature. That mixed model gives us a pitcher's expected contribution, similar to what we do for our DRC+ model for hitters and FRAA model for catchers. (Oh, and we also consider the pitcher's effect on basestealing and on balls getting past the catcher.)

It's important to note that DRA is set to the scale of runs allowed per nine innings (RA9) instead of ERA, which makes DRA's scale slightly higher than ERA's. The reason for this is because ERA tends to overrate three types of pitchers:

1. Pitchers who play in parks where scorers hand out more errors. Official scorers differ significantly in the frequency at which they assign errors to fielders.

2. Ground-ball pitchers, because a substantial proportion of errors occur on grounders.

3. Pitchers who aren't very good. Better pitchers often allow fewer unearned runs than bad pitchers, because good pitchers tend to find ways to get out of jams.

Since the last time you picked up an edition of this book, we've also made a few minor changes to DRA to make it better. Recent research into "tunneling"–the act of throwing consecutive pitches that appear similar from a batter's point of view until after the swing decision point–data has given us a new contextual factor to account for in DRA: plate distance. This refers to the distance between successive pitches as they approach the plate, and while it has a smaller effect than factors like velocity or whiff rate, it still can help explain pitcher strikeout rate in our model.

New Pitching Metrics for 2019

We're including a few "new" pitching metrics for 2019's suite of Baseball Prospectus publications, but you may be familiar with them if you've spent time scouring the internet for stats.

Fastball Percentage

Our fastball percentage (FB%) statistic measures how frequently a pitcher throws a pitch classified as a "fastball," measured as a percentage of overall pitches thrown. We qualify three types of fastballs:

1. The traditional four-seam fastball;
2. The two-seam fastball or sinker;
3. "Hard cutters," which are pitches that have the movement profile of a cut fastball and are used as the pitcher's primary offering or in place of a more traditional fastball.

For example, a pitcher with a FB% of 67 throws any combination of these three pitches about two-thirds of the time.

Whiff Rate

Everybody loves a swing and a miss, and whiff rate (WHF) measures how frequently pitchers induce a swinging strike. To calculate WHF, we add up all the pitches thrown that ended with a swinging strike, then divide that number by a pitcher's total pitches thrown. Most often, high whiff rates correlate with high strikeout rates (and overall effective pitcher performance).

Called Strike Probability

Called Strike Probability (CSP) is a number that represents the likelihood that all of a pitcher's pitches will be called a strike while controlling for location, pitcher and batter handedness, umpire and count. Here's how it works: on each pitch, our model determines how many times (out of 100) that a similar pitch was called for a strike given those factors mentioned above, and when normalized for each batter's strike zone. Then we average the CSP for all pitches thrown by a pitcher in a season, and that gives us the yearly CSP percentage you see in the stats boxes.

As you might imagine, pitchers with a higher CSP are more likely to work in the zone, where pitchers with a lower CSP are likely locating their pitches outside the normal strike zone, for better or for worse.

Projections

Many of you aren't turning to this book just for a look at what a player has done, but for a look at what a player is going to do: the PECOTA projections. PECOTA, initially developed by Nate Silver (who has moved on to greater fame as a political analyst), consists of three parts:

1. Major-league equivalencies, which use minor-league statistics to project how a player will perform in the major leagues;
2. Baseline forecasts, which use weighted averages and regression to the mean to estimate a player's current true talent level; and
3. Aging curves, which uses the career paths of comparable players to estimate how a player's statistics are likely to change over time.

With all those important things covered, let's take a look at what's in the book this year.

Team Prospectus

You bought this book to learn more about your favorite (or maybe least-favorite, who are we to judge?) team, so let's talk about them. After a thoughtful preview of the 2019 season, you'll be presented with our Team Prospectus. This outlines many of the key statistics for each team's 2018 season, as well as a very inviting stadium diagram.

First you'll find the Performance Graphs page. The first is the 2018 Hit List Ranking. This shows our Hit List Rank for the team on each day of the 2018 season and is intended to give you a picture of the ups and downs of the team's season, including their highest and lowest ranks of the year. Hit List Rank measures overall team performance and drives the Hit List Power Rankings at the baseballprospectus.com website.

The second graph is Committed Payroll and helps you see how the team's payroll has compared to the MLB and divisional average payrolls over time. Payroll figures are currents as of January 1, 2019; with so many free agents still unsigned as of this writing, the final 2018 figure will likely be significantly different for many teams. (In the meantime, you can always find the most current data at Baseball Prospectus' Cot's Baseball Contracts page.)

The third graph is Farm System Ranking and displays how the Baseball Prospectus prospect team has ranked the organization's farm system since 2007. It also indicates the highest and lowest ranks that the farm system achieved over that time.

We start the Team Performance page with the squad's unadjusted and third-order 2018 win-loss records, presented in divisional context. We then list the three highest performing hitters and pitchers by WARP for 2018. Beneath that are a host of other team statistics. **Pythag** presents an adjusted 2018 winning percentage, calculated by taking runs scored per game (**RS/G**) and runs allowed per game (**RA/G**) for the team, and running them through a version of Bill James' Pythagorean formula that was refined and improved by David Smyth and Brandon Heipp. (The formula is called "Pythagenpat," which is equally fun to type and to say.)

Next up is **DRC+**, described earlier, to indicate the overall hitting ability of the team either above or below league-average. Run prevention on the pitching side is covered by **DRA** (also mentioned earlier) and another metric: Fielding Independent Pitching (**FIP**), which calculates another ERA-like statistic based on strikeouts, walks, and home runs recorded. Defensive Efficiency Rating (**DER**) tells us the percentage of balls in play turned into outs for the team, and is a quick fielding shorthand that rounds out run prevention.

After that, we have several measures related to roster composition, as opposed to on-field performance. **B-Age** and **P-Age** tell us the average age of a team's batters and pitchers, respectively. **Salary** is the combined team payroll for all on-field players, and Doug Pappas' Marginal Dollars per Marginal Win (**M$/MW**) tells us how much money a team spent to earn production above replacement level.

Ending this batch of statistics is the number of disabled list days a team had over the season (**DL Days**) and the amount of salary paid to players on the disabled list (**$ on DL**); this final number is expressed as a percentage of total payroll.

Next to each of these stats, we've listed each team's MLB rank in that category from 1st to 30th. In this, 1st always indicates a positive outcome and 30th a negative outcome, except in the case of salary–1st is highest.

The Team Projections page is intended to convey the team's operational capacity entering the 2019 season. We start with the team's PECOTA projected record for 2019, again in divisional context. The **+/-** column indicates how many more or less wins the team is projected to get than they got in 2018. We then list the three highest projected hitters and pitchers by WARP for 2018. A brief farm system summary follows, with the team's top prospect and number of BP Top 101 Prospects. Finally, we list the key new players and departed players, along with their 2019 projected WARP.

Alex Bregman   3B

Born: 03/30/94   Age: 25   Bats: R   Throws: R
Height: 6'0"   Weight: 180   Origin: Round 1, 2015 Draft (#2 overall)

YEAR	TEAM	LVL	AGE	PA	R	2B	3B	HR	RBI	BB	K	SB	CS	AVG/OBP/SLG
2016	CCH	AA	22	285	54	16	2	14	46	42	26	5	3	.297/.415/.559
2016	FRE	AAA	22	83	17	6	0	6	15	5	12	2	1	.333/.373/.641
2016	HOU	MLB	22	217	31	13	3	8	34	15	52	2	0	.264/.313/.478
2017	HOU	MLB	23	626	88	39	5	19	71	55	97	17	5	.284/.352/.475
2018	HOU	MLB	24	705	105	51	1	31	103	96	85	10	4	.286/.394/.532
2019	HOU	MLB	25	675	96	38	3	23	78	73	107	12	4	.272/.359/.463

Breakout: 6%   Improve: 52%   Collapse: 5%   Attrition: 2%   MLB: 100%
Comparables: Anthony Rendon, David Wright, Pablo Sandoval

YEAR	TEAM	LVL	AGE	PA	DRC+	VORP	BABIP	BRR	FRAA	WARP
2016	CCH	AA	22	285	172	38.9	.286	1.6	SS(51): -3.4, 3B(11): 1.4	2.7
2016	FRE	AAA	22	83	161	10.0	.333	-1.2	SS(14): 2.1, LF(3): -0.1	0.8
2016	HOU	MLB	22	217	107	9.6	.317	0.5	3B(40): 0.9, SS(6): -0.1	1.1
2017	HOU	MLB	23	626	114	34.7	.311	-1.5	3B(132): 8.7, SS(30): -2.9	3.9
2018	HOU	MLB	24	705	150	72.6	.289	-1.6	3B(136): 5.4, SS(28): -0.4	7.4
2019	HOU	MLB	25	675	125	37.3	.295	0.0	3B 7, SS 0	4.6

After the projections page, we share a few items about the team's home ballpark. There's the aforementioned diagram of the park's dimensions (including distances to the outfield wall), a few important biographical facts about the stadium, a graphic showing the height of the wall from the left-field pole to the right-field pole, and a table showing three-year park factors for the stadium. The park factors are displayed as indexes where 100 is average, 110 means that the park inflates the statistic in question by 10 percent, and 90 means that the park deflates the statistic in question by 10 percent.

Following the ballpark page, we have a **Personnel** section that lists many of the important decision-makers and upper-level field and operations staff members for the franchise, as well as any former Baseball Prospectus staff members who are currently part of the organization.

Position Players

After all that information and a thoughtful bylined essay covering each team, we present our player comments. Each player is listed with the major-league team who employed him as of early January 2019. If a player changed teams after that point via free agency, trade, or any other method, you'll be able to find them in the book for their previous squad.

First, we cover biographical information (age is as of June 30, 2019) before moving onto the stats themselves. Our statistic columns include standard identifying information like **YEAR**, **TEAM**, **LVL** (level of affiliated play) and **AGE** before getting into the numbers. Next, we provide raw, unstranslated numbers like you might find on the back of your dad's baseball cards: **PA** (plate appearances), **R** (runs), **2B** (doubles), **3B** (triples), **HR** (home runs), **RBI** (runs batted in), **BB** (walks), **K** (strikeouts), **SB** (stolen bases) and **CS** (caught stealing). Then we have unadjusted "slash" statistics: **AVG** (batting average), **OBP** (on-base percentage) and **SLG** (slugging percentage).

Just below the stats box is **PECOTA** data, which is discussed further in a following section. After that, it's on to a pithy and always-informative comment written by a member of the Baseball Prospectus staff, before we cover more stats.

The second text box repeats YEAR, TEAM, LVL, AGE, and PA, then moves on to **DRC+** (Deserved Runs Created Plus), which we described earlier as total offensive expected contribution compared to the league average. Next, one of our oldest active metrics, **VORP** (Value Over Replacement Player), considers offensive production, position and plate appearances. In essence, it is the number of runs contributed beyond what a replacement-level player at the same position would contribute if given the same percentage of team plate appearances. VORP does not consider the quality of a player's defense.

BABIP (batting average on balls in play) tells us how often a ball in play fell for a hit, and can help us identify whether a batter may have been lucky or not … but note that high BABIPs also tend to follow the great hitters of our time, as well as speedy singles hitters who put the ball on the ground.

The next item is **BRR** (Baserunning Runs), which covers all of a player's baserunning accomplishments which includes (but isn't limited to) swiped bags and failed attempts. Next is **FRAA** (Fielding Runs Above Average), which also includes the number of games previously played at each position noted in parentheses. Multi-position players have only their two most frequent positions listed here, but their total FRAA number reflects all positions played.

Our last column here is **WARP** (Wins Above Replacement Player). WARP estimates the total value of a player, which means for hitters it takes into account hitting runs above average (calculated using the DRC+ model), BRR and FRAA. Then, it makes an adjustment for positions played and gives the player a credit for plate appearances based upon the difference between "replacement level"¬–which is derived from the quality of players added to a team's roster after the start of the season¬–and the league average.

Catchers

Catchers are a special breed, and thus they have earned their own separate box which displays some of the defensive metrics that we've built just for them. As an example, let's check out J.T. Realmuto.

YEAR	TEAM	P. COUNT	FRM RUNS	BLK RUNS	THRW RUNS	TOT RUNS
2016	MIA	18935	-8.5	1.8	2.1	-5.6
2017	MIA	18959	5.3	1.7	1.0	9.1
2018	MIA	16399	-0.4	0.9	0.1	0.4
2019	PHI	18448	-1.4	1.5	0.7	0.8

The **YEAR** and **TEAM** columns match what you'd find in the other stat box. **P. COUNT** indicates the number of pitches thrown while the catcher was behind the plate, including swinging strikes, fouls, and balls in play. **FRM RUNS** is the total run value the catcher provided (or cost) his team by influencing the umpire to call strikes where other catchers did not. **BLK RUNS** expresses the total run value above or below average for the catcher's ability to prevent wild pitches and passed balls. **THRW RUNS** is calculated using a similar model as the previous two statistics, and it measures a catcher's ability to throw out basestealers but also to dissuade them from testing his arm in the first place. It takes into account factors like the pitcher (including his delivery and pickoff move) and baserunner (who could be as fast as Billy Hamilton or as slow as Yonder Alonso). **TOT RUNS** is the sum of all of the previous three statistics.

Pitchers

Let's give our pitchers a turn, using 2018 NL Cy Young winner Jacob deGrom as our example. Take a look at his first stat block: the first line and the **YEAR**, **TEAM**, **LVL** and **AGE** columns are the same as in the position player example earlier.

Here too, we have a series of columns that display raw, unadjusted statistics compiled by the pitcher over the course of a season: **W** (wins), **L** (losses), **SV** (saves), **G** (games pitched), **GS** (games started), **IP** (innings pitched), **H** (hits allowed) and **HR** (home runs allowed). Next we have two statistics that are rates: **BB/9** (walks per nine innings) and **K/9** (strikeouts per nine innings), before returning to the unadjusted **K** (strikeouts).

Next up is **GB%** (ground ball percentage), which is the percentage of all batted balls that were hit in the ground, including both outs and hits. Remember, this is based on observational data and subject to human error, so please approach this with a healthy dose of skepticism.

BABIP (batting average on balls in play) is calculated using the same methodology as it is for position players, but it often tells us more about a pitcher than it does a hitter. With pitchers, a high BABIP is often due to poor defense or bad luck, and can often be an indicator of potential rebound, and a low BABIP may be cause to expect performance regression. (A typical league-average BABIP is close to .290-.300.)

After a witty 150ish words on the player like only Baseball Prospectus's staff can provide, it's on to that second stat block, which repeats the YEAR, TEAM, LVL, and AGE columns. The metrics **WHIP** (walks plus hits per inning pitched) and **ERA** (earned run average) are old standbys: WHIP measures walks and hits allowed on a per-inning basis, while ERA measures earned runs on a nine-inning basis. Neither of these stats are translated or adjusted.

DRA (Deserved Run Average) was described at length earlier, and measures how many runs the pitcher "deserved" to allow per nine innings. Please note that since we lack all the data points that would make for a "real" DRA for minor-league events, the DRA displayed for minor league partial-seasons is based off of different data. (That data is a modified version of our cFIP metric, which you can find more information about on our website.)

Jacob deGrom RHP

Born: 06/19/88   Age: 31   Bats: L   Throws: R
Height: 6'4"   Weight: 180   Origin: Round 9, 2010 Draft (#272 overall)

YEAR	TEAM	LVL	AGE	W	L	SV	G	GS	IP	H	HR	BB/9	K/9	K	GB%	BABIP
2016	NYN	MLB	28	7	8	0	24	24	148	142	15	2.2	8.7	143	47%	.312
2017	NYN	MLB	29	15	10	0	31	31	201^1	180	28	2.6	10.7	239	48%	.305
2018	NYN	MLB	30	10	9	0	32	32	217	152	10	1.9	11.2	269	48%	.281
2019	NYN	MLB	31	13	9	0	31	31	186	145	18	2.3	10.7	221	46%	.286

Breakout: 8%   Improve: 29%   Collapse: 28%   Attrition: 6%   MLB: 85%
Comparables: Erik Bedard, A.J. Burnett, CC Sabathia

YEAR	TEAM	LVL	AGE	WHIP	ERA	DRA	WARP	MPH	FB%	WHF	CSP
2016	NYN	MLB	28	1.20	3.04	3.30	3.5	96.3	59.6	12.1	47.2
2017	NYN	MLB	29	1.19	3.53	3.02	5.7	97.2	55.5	14.5	49.5
2018	NYN	MLB	30	0.91	1.70	2.09	8.0	98.2	52.1	16.3	48.4
2019	NYN	MLB	31	1.02	2.91	3.23	3.9	96.6	54.5	14.8	48.2

Just like with hitters, **WARP** (Wins Above Replacement Player) is a total value metric that puts pitchers of all stripes on the same scale as position players. We use DRA as the primary input for our calculation of WARP. You might notice that relief pitchers (due to their limited innings) may have a lower WARP than you were expecting or than you might see in other WARP-like metrics. WARP does not take leverage into account, just the actions a pitcher performs and the expected value of those actions ... which ends up judging high-leverage relief pitchers differently than you might imagine given their prestige and market value.

MPH gives you the pitcher's 95th percentile velocity for the noted season, in order to give you an idea of what the *peak* fastball velocity a pitcher possesses. Since this comes from our pitch tracking data, it is not publicly available for minor-league pitchers.

Finally, we display the three new pitching metrics we described earlier. **FB%** (fastball percentage) gives you the percentage of fastballs thrown out of all pitches. **WhiffRt** (whiff rate) tells you the percentage of swinging strikes induced out of all pitches. **CS Prob** (called strike probability) expresses the likelihood of all pitches thrown to result in a called strike, after controlling for factors like handedness, umpire, pitch type, count, and location.

PECOTA

All players have PECOTA projections for 2019, as well as a set of other numbers that describe the performance of comparable players according to PECOTA. All projections for 2019 are for the player at the date we went to press in early January and are projected into the league and park context as indicated by the team abbreviation. All PECOTA projected statistics represent a player's projected major-league performance.

The numbers beneath the player's stats–Breakout, Improve, Collapse, Attrition–are part and parcel of the PECOTA projections. They estimate the likelihood of changes in performance relative to the player's previously-established level of production, based on the performance of comparable players:

Breakout Rate is the percent change that a player's production will improve by at least 20 percent relative to the weighted average of his performance over his most recent seasons.

Improve Rate is the percent chance that a player's production will improve at all relative to his baseline performance. A player who is expected to perform just the same as he has in the recent past will have an Improve Rate of 50 percent.

Collapse Rate is the percent chance that a position player's production will decline by at least 25 percent relative to his baseline performance.

Attrition Rate operates on playing time rather than performance. Specifically, it measures the likelihood that a player's playing time will decrease by at least 50 percent relative to his established level.

Breakout Rate and Collapse Rate can sometimes be counterintuitive for players who have already experienced a radical change in performance level. It's also worth noting that the projected decline in a player's rate performances might not be indicative of an expected decline in underlying ability or skill, but could just be an anticipated correction following a breakout season.

MLB% is the percentage of similar players who played in the major leagues in their relevant season.

The final pieces of information are the player's three highest-scoring comparable players as determined by PECOTA. All comparables represent a snapshot of how the listed player was performing at the same age as the current player, so if a 23-year-old pitcher is compared to Bartolo Colon, he's actually being compared to a 23-year-old Colon, not the version that pitched for the Rangers in 2018, nor to Colon's career as a whole.

A few points about pitcher projections. First, we aren't yet projecting peak velocity, so that column will be blank in the PECOTA lines. Second, projecting DRA is trickier than evaluating past performance, because it is unclear how deserving each pitcher will be of his anticipated outcomes. However, we know that another DRA-related statistic–contextual FIP or cFIP–estimates future run scoring very well. So for PECOTA, the projected DRA figures you see are based on the past cFIPs generated by the pitcher and comparable players over time, along with the other factors described above.

Lineouts

In each chapter's Lineouts section, you'll find abbreviated text comments, as well as most of same information you'd find in our full player comments. We limit the stats boxes in this section to only including the 2018 information for each player.

Exclusive Player Visualizations

In our constant battle to provide you with new and interesting baseball content you can't find anywhere else, we've added a trio of data visualizations to each hitter's entry in these books and a pair of visualizations for each pitcher.

For hitters, you'll find three new infographics. The first is each player's **Batted Ball Distribution**, which displays the five major sections of the field: LF (left), LCF (left center), CF (center), RCF (right center), and RF (right). The percentage indicated tells us what percentage of batted balls from that hitter fell within that part of the field during the 2018 season. We've also included the hitter's slugging percentage on balls in play (also called **SLGCON**) for that part of the field.

You'll also see two heatmaps: **Strike Zone vs LHP** and **Strike Zone vs RHP**. These heat maps represent a view of the strike zone from behind the catcher. Areas where there is a darker coloration represent the places where a higher percentage of pitches resulted in hits. In other words, the heatmap represents a hitter's "sweet spots" for getting hits against either left-handed or right-handed pitchers, depending on the image.

Pitchers get two images that help explain what their pitches look like from a hitter's perspective: **Pitch Shape vs LHH** and **Pitch Shape vs RHH**. These images show you the shape and the "tunneling" effect of each pitcher's offerings from the batter's perspective. For each type of pitch that a pitcher throws (represented by an indicator shape), there's a set of dots indicating the flight path, where each dot represents a 0.01-second interval. This maps the average trajectory and speed of an offering, ending where the ball crosses the plate. The solid black box represents the regular strike zone, while the gray contour lines indicate the range of locations that a pitcher typically works in.

Below the image, we provide a bit more detailed information about each pitcher's average offering in the **Pitch Types** box. Here, we also list each of the pitcher's major offerings under the **Type** column.

- **Fastballs** (which usually refers to the four-seam variation)
- **Sinkers** and/or two-seam fastballs
- **Cutters** (which could include "hard" cutters like cut fastballs and "soft" cutters that resemble hard sliders)
- **Changeups** (not including most splitters)
- **Splitters** (split-fingered pitches, forkballs, and some split-changes)
- **Sliders** and/or slurves
- **Curveballs** (including spike-curveballs and knuckle-curveballs, as well as some slurvy curves)
- **Slow curveballs** and/or eephus pitches
- **Knuckleballs**
- **Screwballs**

The **Freq** column indicates the percentage of overall pitches that fall into each of those type categories; if a pitcher has a 16.55% score for changeups, then that's the percent of all pitches that he throws as changeups. **Velo** is exactly what you think it is: the average miles per hour for each pitch type. **H Mov** is the number of inches of horizontal movement on the average pitch of that type, while **V Mov** is the number of inches of vertical movement on the average pitch of that type. (At Baseball Prospectus, we measure this over the long flight of the ball and include gravity into the V Mov number in order to give you the most realistic representation of what the pitch *actually* does.)

If you're wondering about the second number in brackets, that's the index for that velocity or movement compared to the league average. Like DRC+, a score of 100 means that the speed or movement is about the same as league average, while a higher score means that there's higher velocity or movement than the league average. Numbers below 100 indicate less velocity or movement than the league average.

Part 1: Team Analysis

Part II: Team Analysis

Table for Two: Previewing the 2019 Detroit Tigers

Patrick Dubuque and Matt Sussman

MATT SUSSMAN: We are all aware the Tigers are among the precisely 87 teams currently rebuilding. They stand out primarily due to their sudden shift from perennial American League contender to mid-Michigan's spiciest garage sale, and this was always part of the deal in 2012—that 2018 was going to hurt. They planned to dive underwater before it was cool to drown. But the method no longer matters. They're indistinguishable from the rest of the flotsam, with the exception that an active Hall of Famer exists on the payroll.

It's a very different team with Miguel Cabrera swinging a stick in the nucleus of the lineup. Another injury, or if the biceps didn't heal correctly, and suddenly the lineup rallies around Nick Castellanos, who will rack up extra base hits in between photoshopping himself in various other uniforms, half for morbid curiosity and half to know what he'll be doing in August. Is there anything else remotely neat to say about the lineup?

PATRICK DUBUQUE: I feel guilty even talking about these hitters. This lineup is an episode of "Remember Some Guys" except the answer is "No." This isn't one of those situations where you let the kids play even though they're not ready, let them take some licks… this is what happens when you don't even have enough kids to do that. Other than the two guys you mentioned, no Tigers hitter is projected to be above-average by DRC+ except recent recruit Josh Harrison, and it's hard to imagine many of them being on the next Important Tigers team. There is nothing to remember about the 2019 Detroit Tigers. I could write literally anything to end this paragraph, confess to a grisly string of murders, and your brain would forget every word you just read.

This isn't fair to Jeimer Candelario, the one guy not already mentioned whose name can't be used as a sedative. If my interest in the 2019 Detroit Tigers were a currency, I would invest every penny of it into watching Candelario develop, not because I think he'll be a star, but because he's the only bat in this lineup who might still be around the next time the team gets to 82 wins. It's a good thing pitchers are wildly volatile, just so you can't set your watch to their mediocrity. Does anyone give you hope on the pitching side?

MATT: Dare I say it? The bullpen might be… what's the word for "opposite of bad?" Sorry, this is new to all of us. Joe Jimenez finally became the closer prospect that panned out. Blaine Hardy keeps the ball in the park and Victor Alcantara finally looked up "what is a strike zone" on Wikipedia. But all those years of doing nothing but recruiting hard-throwing SEC righthanders with SP3 ceilings may pay dividends in the form of their floor, a mid-2010s Orioles-style competent pen. Drew VerHagen, Buck Farmer, Spencer Turnbull, and (coming soon) Kyle Funkhouser could lead the way to Jimenez (or Shane Greene for now). That's not nothing, and the the Leyland-era Tigers can't say that.

Through it all, the bullpen might be this team's emerging strength, and it shouldn't be a team's only strength, hence the pessimism and ennui, but the less they need to ride the bullpen cart in the fourth inning, the better. The hardest part of an organizational demo job is watching decent pitchers being stretched beyond their ability, ballooning their ERAs. Do they have enough in the rotation to avoid that?

PATRICK: No.

I mean, not that it matters, right? I guess the games have to end, so someone has to mark the time. But it's hard to imagine veterans like Zimmermann, Ross or Moore enjoying memories of arm strength past to the point where they create value at the trade deadline. Fullmer you're literally rooting to survive, which leaves Daniel Norris (whom PECOTA is optimistic about, thanks to a spike in K% despite losing a lot of velocity) as the only bellwether for a successful 2019.

So by my count you've got two, maybe three guys on the Opening Day roster that qualify as legitimately interesting, at least from a "fate of the franchise" perspective. This is a problem, and one I intend to solve through a meticulously-crafted strategy called "Don't Watch the Tigers." What are you going to do, Matt?

MATT: Go against doctor's orders, per usual. It might not be *that* bad. Last year I went in with the lowest of expectations and a 98-loss season was surprisingly watchable. Ron Gardenhire-branded teams have consistently turned lemons into one-run losses. The players made some immature, lunkheaded decisions all over the diamond but on the whole played hard and it might not win games but keeps you tuned in.

But I won't blame if you if you decide to sit this one out, at least attentively. Even for the broadcast purposes, the TV crew is brand new (after Mario Impemba and Rod Allen argued about a chair or maybe not, ending their 16-year detente) and not necessarily improved. Matt Shepard is perfectly serviceable, but the presence of Kirk Gibson and Jack Morris is simply for kitsch value. They may as well have promoted the Packard Automotive Plant to be the color commentator. For those in Michigan, put it on the radio and listen to the vastly underrated Dan Dickerson while you're putting together your kid's bicycle, trying to get the wheel in, crying that you can't get the wheel in, reevaluating all your parenting skills, wishing the bicycle had never been invented, and then suddenly hear the radio call of JaCoby Jones rounding second and what in the world is he doing, now he's in a rundown.

PATRICK: We're reaching perilously close to the theme song of the 2019 offseason, but never more often in recent memory have we witnessed so many stories where we already know the ending. This team has the feel of a Yoko Ono movie, more about how the audience copes with the experience of sitting through the movie than the film itself. So it's natural to turn attention to the minors, and looking at the Top 10 Prospect List, a lot of those names have projected ETAs of late 2019. Does it feel like the pieces of the next good Tigers team are on their way? Is this team preview going to be more fun to write next year?

MATT: Having watched much more Triple-A baseball, because who can blame me, a few of those fellas have potential to steal playing time. Daz Cameron comes to mind first. Mike's kid should be the everyday center fielder in 2020 to make us feel both optimistic and old. Funkhouser, I mentioned before, perhaps because I just want to see a pitcher named Funkhouser. I'd like to see Jake Rogers sooner rather than later because the team cut James McCann loose, rightly so, and the catcher depth in the organization has been annoyingly thin—so bleak, in fact, the GM just had his son do it a couple times.

They say Casey Mize might be ready this year? Seems rushed but everything I've read about the last year's first overall pick means he's a mature player and I know exactly why I'm conditioned to not be excited. It's because I fully expect Dave Dombrowski to trade him for a setup man because I still feel like it's 2013.

Gardenhire will get the most out of all of them. I don't know if most these players will become the winning team of the future. But that's how rebuilds go. The entire process is frustrating, because they ask the fans to he patient, as if, what are you going to do if we don't? As long as MLB At Bat exists, well sidewatch whatever team we damn well please, Verlander and Scherzer and J.D. and all the other Motor City alumni excel with winning teams and also the Nationals, and when the local team is back on top, we'll watch again. No, Tigers, *you* be patient. We'll be realistic.

So how realistic are we going to be? Detroit replicated 2017's struggles with another 64-win season. PECOTA has them at 67. I'll just say 64 again just for the Khris Davis-like consistency of doing something weird exactly the same way three times in a row. What say you?

PATRICK: For all my jokes, I'm actually a little optimistic about this year's Tigers, in the sense that I'd lean toward 70 wins rather than 64. My logic isn't that any of these players is particularly primed for a breakout, but that, especially offensively, there are so many open competitions that one, statistically speaking, is likely to happen. Maybe it's Cameron or one of the rookies allowed to start their clock early, or maybe it's one of those March 31, last-cut-on-a-better-roster guys who washes up on Detroit's shores. Someone will almost certainly be good for the Tigers this year.

Enjoy finding out which one!

Performance Graphs

2018 Hit List Ranking

Lowest rank: 26   Highest rank: 13

Committed Payroll (in millions)

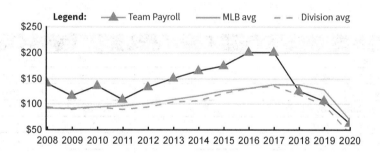

Legend: ▲ Team Payroll   —— MLB avg   – – Division avg

Farm System Ranking

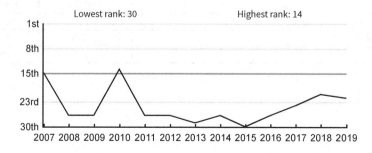

Lowest rank: 30   Highest rank: 14

2018 Team Performance

ACTUAL STANDINGS

Team	W	L	Pct
CLE	91	71	.561
MIN	78	84	.481
DET	**64**	**98**	**.395**
CHA	62	100	.382
KCA	58	104	.358

THIRD-ORDER STANDINGS

Team	W	L	Pct
CLE	92	70	.567
MIN	70	92	.432
DET	**62**	**100**	**.382**
CHA	61	101	.376
KCA	58	104	.358

TOP HITTERS

Player	WARP
Nick Castellanos	3.5
Jose Iglesias	2.3
Niko Goodrum	0.9

TOP PITCHERS

Player	WARP
Joe Jimenez	1.4
Blaine Hardy	1.2
Michael Fulmer	1

VITAL STATISTICS

Statistic Name	Value	Rank
Pythagenpat	.393	26th
Runs Scored per Game	3.89	26th
Runs Allowed per Game	4.91	23rd
Deserved Runs Created Plus	89	25th
Deserved Run Average	4.77	23rd
Fielding Independent Pitching	4.62	25th
Defensive Efficiency Rating	.709	10th
Batter Age	27.9	13th
Pitcher Age	28.7	17th
Salary	$125.3M	19th
Marginal $ per Marginal Win	$7.3M	4th
Disabled List Days	$865.0M	6th
$ on DL	24%	26th

2019 Team Projections

PROJECTED STANDINGS

Team	W	L	Pct	+/-
CLE	97	65	.598	+6
MIN	82	80	.506	+4
KCA	72	90	.444	+14
CHA	70	92	.432	+8
DET	**67**	**95**	**.413**	**+3**

TOP PROJECTED HITTERS

Player	WARP
Miguel Cabrera	2.5
Nick Castellanos	1.9
Josh Harrison	1.4

TOP PROJECTED PITCHERS

Player	WARP
Michael Fulmer	2.3
Daniel Norris	1.1
Matt Boyd	0.9

FARM SYSTEM REPORT

Top Prospect	Number of Top 101 Prospects
Casey Mize, #36	1

KEY DEDUCTIONS

Player	WARP
Jose Iglesias	1.4
Francisco Liriano	0.4

KEY ADDITIONS

Player	WARP
Josh Harrison	1.4
Jordy Mercer	0.7
Matt Moore	0.3
Tyson Ross	0.3

Team Personnel

EVP, General Manager
Al Avila

VP, Assistant General Manager
David Chadd

VP, Assistant General Manager
John Westhoff

Manager
Ron Gardenhire

Comerica Park Stats

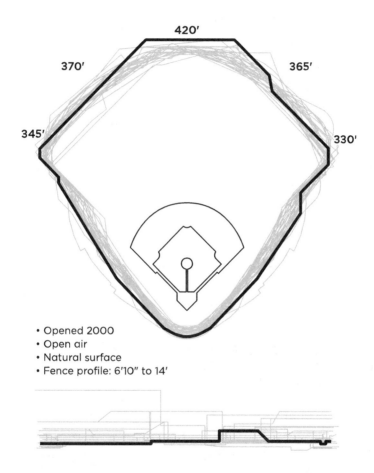

420'

370'   365'

345'   330'

- Opened 2000
- Open air
- Natural surface
- Fence profile: 6'10" to 14'

Three-Year Park Factors

Runs	Runs/RH	Runs/LH	HR/RH	HR/LH
102	103	99	102	104

Tigers Team Analysis

"**H**ow long are you willing to wait?"

"It's supposed to be really, really great. Everybody said they loved it, even though—yeah, it's going to take forever."

"So, get in line?"

"I think we have to."

Contemporary baseball decision-makers have lured fans into the mindset that fuels amusement parks: There's this ride. You're going to wait for it, bored and sweaty and not amused at all, but look at those people coming out the other side, smiling. It's all on purpose, all *worth it*. The euphoria, glimpsed vividly in several recent Novembers, sticks with people and provides license to start the whole process over; the all-important rush makes the next wait feel not just shorter, but *necessary*.

ⓧ　　ⓧ　　ⓧ

The 2018 Tigers didn't come close to mirroring the historically putrid 2003 Tigers, finishing third in a veritable wasteland of a division, but they existed in the same non-competitive fugue state that characterized the early Dave Dombrowski years in Detroit. However, their paths forward are unlikely to be similar.

The popular justification for suffering through terrible teams wasn't stated in its current form back then, and Tigers owner Mike Ilitch, who died in 2017, was refreshingly impatient with losing. Ilitch and Dombrowski dropped serious dollars on Ivan Rodriguez that winter, and on Magglio Ordonez the next offseason. They pumped money into the team in what many, today, would call "confusing" or "inefficient" moves that created incongruence between the utility of the highly paid stars and the young talent.

In 2006, Rodriguez and Ordonez were aging and merely average players, but Justin Verlander and Curtis Granderson arrived on the scene. That wasn't nearly enough to produce the World Series berth, though. Several other things were required. Namely:

- Jeremy Bonderman put forth his only good season.
- A 41-year-old Kenny Rogers signed for two years (two years!) and $16 million, pitching about as well as anyone could have reasonably hoped.

- Carlos Guillen put up a career-year at age 30, two years after being acquired for a prospect who'd never pan out and Ramon Santiago—who was already back on the Tigers after being released by the Mariners.
- Oh, and Brandon Inge posted a five-WARP season at third base.

None of those things held up. The team's main window of contention came later, after a couple more top-10 picks turned into Miguel Cabrera via trade. The Tigers, at that point, had officially reached the front of the line.

⚾   ⚾   ⚾

Even that Cabrera-led team didn't take off immediately, but the Tigers eventually ripped off four straight postseason appearances, including one trip to the World Series. Yet all of their Octobers ended in dry, quiet clubhouses. If hoisting the trophy was the payoff, then did Detroit wait for nothing? The notion feels blindingly dishonest.

Every other fan base has been waiting decades to see a Triple Crown winner. Certainly fans accepting a tanking plan would happily put in a wait to see such a thing. How long would you wait to see a pitching season so dominant it earned the Cy Young and MVP awards? Only the Dodgers have had the pleasure of seeing a season like Verlander's 2011 this millennium, and only the A's saw it in the 1990s. What amount of time is paid off by the chance to relish two Hall of Fame peaks fully and simultaneously? Since the strike, only the Yankees (pick your timeframe), the Braves of Chipper Jones, Tom Glavine and company, and the Tigers of Cabrera and Verlander are solid bets for multiple Cooperstown trips.

Those designations were all subject to the whims of the universe, deserved to differing degrees. Day by day, they become decreasingly relevant to the happiness of those who attach their feelings to a baseball team. It's true of a World Series win, too, but there is undeniably a greater release achieved when that trophy is handed over—one that Ilitch so clearly wanted, and that everyone around the team wanted for him.

In that sense, the gloom of the early 2000s and pre-Ilitch 1990s (when famed Michigan college football coach Bo Schembechler inexplicably ran the team) appear to be an interminable procession toward thrills set to fade in a fraction of the time.

⚾   ⚾   ⚾

Winning without *really* winning can feel like a singular, crushing sequence of events, mostly because of recent history's recency. It may remain crushing, but it won't be singular.

The Nationals have developed a talent pipeline that looks likely to keep their contention window open, but they exhausted the control years of Stephen Strasburg and Bryce Harper without winning a postseason series. The Pirates are toiling at transforming their roster for a longer haul, but just watched their former no. 1 overall pick, Gerrit Cole, go supernova in a different uniform.

The Braves, the Phillies, the White Sox, the post-championship Royals—some of these rebuilds are going to come up empty. This isn't a science despite the Cubs' and Astros' triumphant whole-hog teardowns. But the top-line disappointment of Detroit's last competitive cycle made for an easy reason to do things differently this time around. General manager Al Avila, embarking on his mission in 2016 after replacing Dombrowski, said he needed to make the club younger and leaner (read: cheaper).

So far, he's moving steadily along, staying within the roped-off path. They had the no. 1 overall pick in June, taking Auburn right-hander Casey Mize. They will have the no. 5 pick in the 2019 draft. A few prospects acquired in the sell-off have begun to pop, like Daz Cameron (son of Mike, acquired for Verlander) and Isaac Paredes (an infielder who came over from the Cubs). There's a void in premium position-player talent, but it's too early to be too worried; uncertainty is always going to be present in this phase of talent collection.

Still, it's worth noting that the biggest trade chips are used up, unless they plan to make the wait longer and the expectations subliminally bigger by dealing Michael Fulmer, a 26-year-old former first-round pick who was acquired as a prospect from the Mets for Yoenis Cespedes in mid-2015. The fact that it could end up looking like a good idea is reminder enough of why Ilitch and Dombrowski stalled as long as they could: Going to the back of the line is daunting.

Someone, multiple someones, eventually decided take the plunge. *I think we have to.*

𐀁   𐀁   𐀁

But what if they didn't have to?

Say the Tigers had pursued a middle ground. They won't ever reach the carefree, uncommitted financial state of the pre-2018 Phillies or White Sox. They have Cabrera signed for huge money through 2023 and Jordan Zimmermann signed through 2020. In one fell swoop, they shaved 2017's top-tier $199.7 million Opening Day payroll to $125.3 million in 2018. After the 2018 season, another $24 million came off the books where the contracts of Victor Martinez and Jose Iglesias used to reside.

Could they have squeezed J.D. Martinez into the team's immediate and middle-term future with a backloaded deal? The $125 million payroll range could still have been achieved, just one year later, with a step in between. Even if Martinez didn't choose to stay—he seemed to really enjoy his first season in

Boston, after all—might the draft-pick compensation have outstripped the trade return from Arizona? Might a commitment to Martinez have allowed them to turn the less established (but more controllable) Nicholas Castellanos into a trade chip for teams even more committed to restricting payroll?

It's become easier for front offices to sell good odds of being formidable in the future rather than middling with continuous chances of at least seeing October in the present. Stated differently, it sounds downright weird: Their job security is stronger if they lose indiscriminately for a few years.

What the tanking pitch fails to account for is the crowding on this recently blazed path to the bottom. Just as a glut of teams that "can never rebuild" will always end with multiple teams failing miserably, a bevy of teams that "gear up for the long term" will likely lead to multiple teams missing their marks. That's not to say the Tigers are destined to be standing up when the music stops, but someone surely will be.

There are other ways for the Tigers to escape or accelerate the procession, and they may well do it at some point—perhaps another Ivan Rodriguez-like signing, before the team is "ready" for such a move, or maybe a Dombrowski-like trade that packages multiple pieces for an in-his-prime mega-star. That doesn't change the questionable, financially driven decisions to hemorrhage talent and reasons to care without adding much intrigue up ahead.

At the start, rebuilding is accepted as an unquestioned, blank-check explanation, before everyone realizes what they've signed up for. Before the winding path ahead is even in view. The team was not obligated to join the increasingly long line of intentional losing any more than they are obligated to stay in it.

⚾   ⚾   ⚾

There are obvious benefits to decreasing the urgency of tomorrow's game. It opens opportunities for otherwise overlooked contributors, to build depth that can help support and eventually retain generational stars. That mindset can manifest in many forms, and doesn't require a bare-bones roster to flourish. Would employing J.D. Martinez or a third solid starting pitcher have eliminated the 40-man spot used to add discarded former Twins minor leaguer Niko Goodrum? Or blocked Joe Jimenez from running with a setup role?

Goodrum's average-hitting season in a super-utility role could be an aberration, or it could be the start of a useful career as a productive, flexible lineup stopgap. Jimenez may be the last Tigers All-Star you remember in a Sporcle quiz in 10 years, or he may be a contributor to the next Tigers contender. They are threads worth pulling on, and that's at least half the battle. Finding them, however, does not require clearing the deck of other attractions. Fans can justifiably wish young seasons were given as much chance to surprise as young careers. It's not too much to ask for a team to remain interesting through May.

While Ilitch's praiseworthy stewardship was sustaining consistent hope for a decade, other teams were mastering the rationalization of mind-numbing slogs through irrelevance. Detroit has arrived at the start again, enticed by this shiny sales pitch, but with no guarantee they're waiting for anything better than the 1990s. How Avila and company feel about the modern safety net of rebuilding, as opposed to the pins and needles of trying, well, that's a question that will define the next few years—and with it the rest of Cabrera's career, Fulmer's future in Detroit, etc.

History provides hope that the Tigers will reach for more than the basic rebuild, maybe sense opportunity in a down division. Even a return to some approximation of the Ordonez days could inspire envy in rival fans spending summer after summer dredging up muddy, metallic objects like Goodrum or Jimenez, telling themselves it's the only way. Those little joys are great, but they're anticipatory, pinned to promised memories from the future. Trying to sustain yourself on them is a fool's errand, like waiting for a ride that may never come.

—Zach Crizer is an author of Baseball Prospectus.

Part 2: Player Analysis

Miguel Cabrera   1B

Born: 04/18/83   Age: 36   Bats: R   Throws: R
Height: 6'4"   Weight: 249   Origin: International Free Agent, 1999

YEAR	TEAM	LVL	AGE	PA	R	2B	3B	HR	RBI	BB	K	SB	CS	AVG/OBP/SLG
2016	DET	MLB	33	679	92	31	1	38	108	75	116	0	0	.316/.393/.563
2017	DET	MLB	34	529	50	22	0	16	60	54	110	0	1	.249/.329/.399
2018	DET	MLB	35	157	17	11	0	3	22	22	27	0	0	.299/.395/.448
2019	DET	MLB	36	564	66	28	2	17	70	69	107	0	0	.273/.365/.443

Breakout: 0%   Improve: 18%   Collapse: 24%   Attrition: 8%   MLB: 91%
Comparables: Paul Konerko, Mark Teixeira, Vladimir Guerrero

If you learned nothing about Cabrera last year, you may have at least discovered that "biceps" is the singular version, not "bicep." That torn muscle is what kept him shelved for most of 2018, and with the biceps' mythical and physical link to power, the oft-hobbled Cabrera's career is finally starting to dovetail into a precarious roster dilemma. A torn biceps is not a common baseball injury — Dean Palmer had one early in his career, and he overcame it — and while Miggy could very well recover from this, there's always concern about the next one. When healthy, the future Hall of Famer is still a patient, intelligent hitter who can drive the ball to all fields. Given those concerns, it's high time to box him into what he does best and DH him more often than not. Cabrera, who'll turn 36 years old in April, is signed through his age-41 season in 2024 and is still owed at least $162 million.

YEAR	TEAM	LVL	AGE	PA	DRC+	VORP	BABIP	BRR	FRAA	WARP
2016	DET	MLB	33	679	153	36.2	.336	-3.8	1B(147): 3.4, 3B(1): -0.1	5.3
2017	DET	MLB	34	529	103	-1.3	.292	-6.6	1B(115): -1.7	0.1
2018	DET	MLB	35	157	108	7.1	.352	0.5	1B(32): 0.0	0.4
2019	DET	MLB	36	564	123	23.4	.316	-1.1	1B -1	2.5

Miguel Cabrera, continued

Batted Ball Distribution

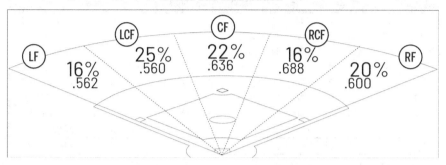

Strike Zone vs LHP   ### Strike Zone vs RHP

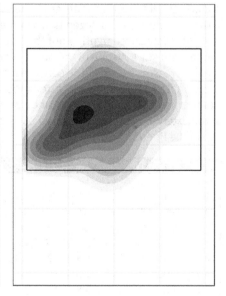

Jeimer Candelario 3B

Born: 11/24/93   Age: 25   Bats: B   Throws: R
Height: 6'1"   Weight: 221   Origin: International Free Agent, 2010

YEAR	TEAM	LVL	AGE	PA	R	2B	3B	HR	RBI	BB	K	SB	CS	AVG/OBP/SLG
2016	TEN	AA	22	244	30	17	1	4	23	32	46	0	0	.219/.324/.367
2016	CHN	MLB	22	14	0	0	0	0	0	2	5	0	0	.091/.286/.091
2016	IOW	AAA	22	309	44	22	3	9	54	38	53	0	2	.333/.417/.542
2017	CHN	MLB	23	36	2	2	0	1	3	1	12	0	0	.152/.222/.303
2017	IOW	AAA	23	330	39	27	3	12	52	41	72	0	0	.266/.361/.507
2017	TOL	AAA	23	128	13	9	1	3	19	5	32	1	0	.264/.297/.430
2017	DET	MLB	23	106	16	7	0	2	13	12	18	0	0	.330/.406/.468
2018	DET	MLB	24	619	78	28	3	19	54	66	160	3	2	.224/.317/.393
2019	DET	MLB	25	468	56	23	2	13	48	42	110	1	1	.242/.318/.400

Breakout: 14%   Improve: 59%   Collapse: 8%   Attrition: 18%   MLB: 96%
Comparables: Jake Lamb, Kyle Seager, Cody Asche

Candelario is going to be a solid contributor hitting somewhere in the lower five spots in the lineup. Out of necessity he started 100 games at leadoff or second in 2018, and more than a dozen times in the cleanup spot. His team was bad, you see. Pitchers started figuring out the switch-hitter after a solid .275/.367/.526 two-month start. As one of the only decent bats in the Tigers' lineup, he chased and he pressed. There's little concern for his defense, at least compared to his positional predecessor Nick Castellanos. And the fact that he crushed nearly 20 homers in a full season shows Candelario can handle the day-to-day grind to some extent. Pencil him in at third base for a while, just don't expect him at the top of the lineup.

YEAR	TEAM	LVL	AGE	PA	DRC+	VORP	BABIP	BRR	FRAA	WARP
2016	TEN	AA	22	244	100	4.2	.261	0.0	3B(54): 2.7, 1B(2): -0.3	0.6
2016	CHN	MLB	22	14	74	-0.5	.167	0.2	3B(3): -0.4	0.0
2016	IOW	AAA	22	309	163	40.9	.383	1.7	3B(67): -0.8, 1B(10): 1.1	2.8
2017	CHN	MLB	23	36	98	-1.1	.200	0.2	3B(9): 0.9, 1B(1): 0.0	0.2
2017	IOW	AAA	23	330	127	23.4	.315	-4.5	3B(70): 5.0, 1B(16): -0.7	1.7
2017	TOL	AAA	23	128	79	1.1	.333	-1.9	3B(28): -1.5	-0.4
2017	DET	MLB	23	106	95	6.9	.392	0.2	3B(27): -2.4	0.1
2018	DET	MLB	24	619	91	16.8	.279	-2.4	3B(140): -4.1	0.9
2019	DET	MLB	25	468	99	10.4	.296	-0.7	3B -1	0.8

Jeimer Candelario, continued

Batted Ball Distribution

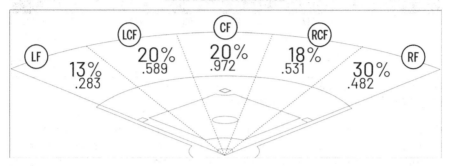

Strike Zone vs LHP   Strike Zone vs RHP

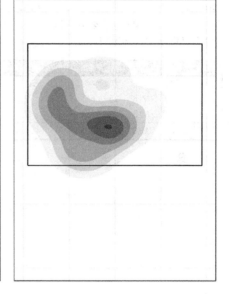

Nick Castellanos   RF

Born: 03/04/92   Age: 27   Bats: R   Throws: R
Height: 6'4"   Weight: 203   Origin: Round 1, 2010 Draft (#44 overall)

YEAR	TEAM	LVL	AGE	PA	R	2B	3B	HR	RBI	BB	K	SB	CS	AVG/OBP/SLG
2016	DET	MLB	24	447	54	25	4	18	58	28	111	1	1	.285/.331/.496
2017	DET	MLB	25	665	73	36	10	26	101	41	142	4	5	.272/.320/.490
2018	DET	MLB	26	678	88	46	5	23	89	49	151	2	1	.298/.354/.500
2019	DET	MLB	27	596	67	35	4	19	76	46	130	3	2	.270/.331/.455

Breakout: 1%   Improve: 46%   Collapse: 16%   Attrition: 5%   MLB: 94%
Comparables: Del Ennis, Shawn Green, Harold Baines

Castellanos is a terrific hitter, but it feels slightly misleading to call him one of
the league's best right fielders. It's kind of like calling your mom's house your
favorite restaurant. More accurately, he's a breakout middle-of-the-lineup hitter
who just happens to be standing in right field on defense. He's a larval
designated hitter still spry enough to play the field (and, as of last year, shared a
roster with Victor Martinez). Third base didn't work out and right field isn't going
much better. He could perhaps operate first base, the last bastion of dudes who
rake but can't bag, but as long as defense matters, Nick the Stick couldn't be a
more accurate moniker.

YEAR	TEAM	LVL	AGE	PA	DRC+	VORP	BABIP	BRR	FRAA	WARP
2016	DET	MLB	24	447	113	18.4	.345	-3.9	3B(108): -3.3	1.5
2017	DET	MLB	25	665	110	22.6	.313	-2.6	3B(129): -7.7, RF(21): -6.0	1.4
2018	DET	MLB	26	678	124	47.6	.361	3.4	RF(142): -2.8	3.5
2019	DET	MLB	27	596	115	25.5	.324	-1.0	RF -5	1.9

Nick Castellanos, continued

Batted Ball Distribution

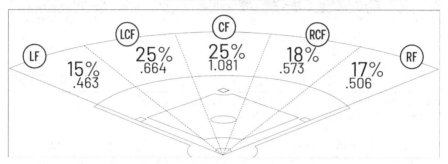

Strike Zone vs LHP   ### Strike Zone vs RHP

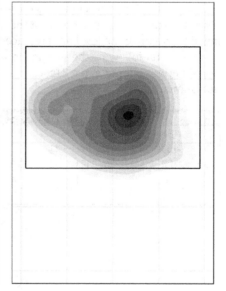

Brandon Dixon 2B

Born: 01/29/92   Age: 27   Bats: R   Throws: R
Height: 6'2"   Weight: 215   Origin: Round 3, 2013 Draft (#92 overall)

YEAR	TEAM	LVL	AGE	PA	R	2B	3B	HR	RBI	BB	K	SB	CS	AVG/OBP/SLG
2016	PEN	AA	24	461	61	23	1	16	65	30	137	15	5	.260/.315/.434
2017	LOU	AAA	25	491	58	31	3	16	64	37	125	18	8	.264/.327/.457
2018	LOU	AAA	26	193	28	18	2	6	23	12	54	9	3	.346/.389/.570
2018	CIN	MLB	26	124	14	6	0	5	10	6	43	0	0	.178/.218/.356
2019	DET	MLB	27	133	15	7	1	4	15	7	39	3	1	.236/.280/.407

Breakout: 3%   Improve: 15%   Collapse: 9%   Attrition: 16%   MLB: 32%
Comparables: Ben Paulsen, Russ Canzler, Zach Walters

In 2018, Brandon Dixon, a longtime theatrical actor and producer, played the role of Judas in NBC's live-action production of *Jesus Christ Superstar*, earning a Primetime Emmy nomination for his portrayal. In 2018, Brandon Dixon, a mildly-toolsy prospect with serious contact issues, played the role of Reds part-time first baseman while Joey Votto recovered from a lower-leg contusion. It's hard to discern which performance was more of a betrayal. A high strikeout rate has always portended struggles against the highest quality arms for Dixon, but he failed to live up to the low bar of replacement level. After being booted off the 40-man roster following the season, he was thrown to the Tigers (which will hopefully work better in the 21st century baseball sense than in the Roman-era punishment sense).

YEAR	TEAM	LVL	AGE	PA	DRC+	VORP	BABIP	BRR	FRAA	WARP
2016	PEN	AA	24	461	107	28.9	.342	2.0	2B(62): 1.0, CF(20): -2.7	0.5
2017	LOU	AAA	25	491	113	22.3	.328	1.0	3B(93): 5.2, 1B(17): -0.3	2.0
2018	LOU	AAA	26	193	158	23.0	.467	2.9	1B(14): 0.1, 2B(14): -2.3	1.5
2018	CIN	MLB	26	124	68	-5.4	.229	-0.5	1B(27): 0.0, RF(17): -1.1	-0.5
2019	DET	MLB	27	133	90	1.9	.311	0.2	1B 0, 3B 0	0.2

Brandon Dixon, continued

Batted Ball Distribution

Strike Zone vs LHP	*Strike Zone vs RHP*

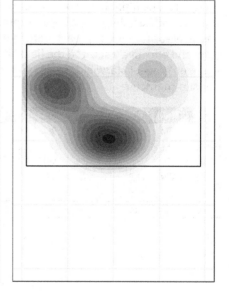

Niko Goodrum   UT

Born: 02/28/92   Age: 27   Bats: B   Throws: R
Height: 6'3"   Weight: 198   Origin: Round 2, 2010 Draft (#71 overall)

YEAR	TEAM	LVL	AGE	PA	R	2B	3B	HR	RBI	BB	K	SB	CS	AVG/OBP/SLG
2016	FTM	A+	24	26	3	4	0	1	5	1	7	1	0	.280/.308/.560
2016	CHT	AA	24	207	25	10	2	6	28	22	52	8	2	.275/.357/.451
2017	ROC	AAA	25	499	71	25	5	13	66	30	119	11	7	.265/.309/.425
2017	MIN	MLB	25	18	1	0	0	0	0	1	10	0	0	.059/.111/.059
2018	DET	MLB	26	492	55	29	3	16	53	42	132	12	4	.245/.315/.432
2019	DET	MLB	27	167	19	8	1	5	19	13	43	4	1	.237/.299/.401

Breakout: 6%   Improve: 49%   Collapse: 14%   Attrition: 16%   MLB: 86%
Comparables: Ryan Flaherty, Dan Uggla, Luke Hughes

Goodrum, a longtime Twins organizational soldier who joined the Tigers on a minor-league deal, took the lingering question mark surrounding his hit tool and deposited it into the right field seats, breaking out with a career-high in home runs for any season of his pro career. Ending camp last year as the Tigers' utility man, he ultimately won the regular second baseman job midseason and the club will keep his versatility as a contingency option. As a switch-hitter, he has an all-or-nothing approach batting lefty (15 of his homers were from that side) and effectively sprayed the field hitting right-handed. He's basically a younger, greener Marwin Gonzalez with a name more suited for an Agatha Christie character.

YEAR	TEAM	LVL	AGE	PA	DRC+	VORP	BABIP	BRR	FRAA	WARP
2016	FTM	A+	24	26	98	3.0	.353	-0.3	SS(2): 0.1, CF(2): -0.2	0.0
2016	CHT	AA	24	207	121	12.3	.352	0.9	3B(24): 1.6, SS(12): 2.6	1.3
2017	ROC	AAA	25	499	99	17.8	.326	4.4	RF(47): 3.3, 2B(37): -4.2	0.9
2017	MIN	MLB	25	18	48	-2.9	.143	0.2	2B(8): -0.4, RF(1): 0.0	-0.1
2018	DET	MLB	26	492	98	12.2	.312	-1.3	2B(64): 1.0, 1B(37): -0.8	0.9
2019	DET	MLB	27	167	88	2.4	.286	0.2	2B -1, 1B 0	0.2

Niko Goodrum, continued

Batted Ball Distribution

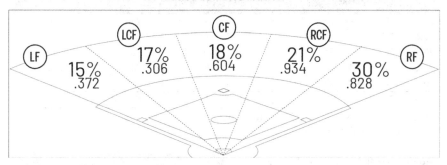

Strike Zone vs LHP   ## Strike Zone vs RHP

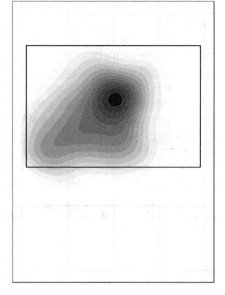

Grayson Greiner   C

Born: 10/11/92   Age: 26   Bats: R   Throws: R
Height: 6'6"   Weight: 239   Origin: Round 3, 2014 Draft (#99 overall)

YEAR	TEAM	LVL	AGE	PA	R	2B	3B	HR	RBI	BB	K	SB	CS	AVG/OBP/SLG
2016	LAK	A+	23	123	14	6	0	0	12	12	26	0	0	.312/.385/.367
2016	ERI	AA	23	225	20	9	3	7	30	10	55	1	0	.288/.320/.462
2017	ERI	AA	24	371	34	20	1	14	42	38	72	0	0	.241/.323/.436
2018	TOL	AAA	25	180	12	8	1	4	23	21	42	0	0	.266/.350/.405
2018	DET	MLB	25	116	9	6	0	0	12	17	32	0	1	.219/.328/.281
2019	DET	MLB	26	344	35	14	2	7	33	34	89	1	0	.223/.302/.351

Breakout: 7%   Improve: 26%   Collapse: 10%   Attrition: 28%   MLB: 54%
Comparables: Tim Federowicz, Rob Bowen, Curtis Casali

Imagine being blessed with great height as well as uncanny athletic ability, and then you use that large frame to ... crouch down for half the game. Greiner is the first 6-foot-6 dude to play catcher in the majors since Pete Koegel for the 1972 Phillies, and only the fourth such player on record. (He's also the first Grayson in the majors since the Chester A. Arthur administration.) Greiner already has more major-league starts at catcher than anyone that tall in history, by far, and that was just in his rookie season. Hopefully you're sitting down while reading this, but it may come as a shock that there's no real height advantage in catching and, some would insist, several disadvantages. He's certainly better at the plate, where the large frame has helped him establish hard contact more often than the league average, though the surface-level numbers didn't quite show that. One could say that his offensive numbers crouched down.

YEAR	TEAM	P. COUNT	FRM RUNS	BLK RUNS	THRW RUNS	TOT RUNS
2017	ERI	12250	22.4	5.5	0.2	27.3
2018	DET	4428	-0.6	-0.2	0.0	-0.9
2018	TOL	6014	9.5	0.5	0.3	10.0
2019	DET	12859	7.3	2.6	-0.7	9.2

YEAR	TEAM	LVL	AGE	PA	DRC+	VORP	BABIP	BRR	FRAA	WARP
2016	LAK	A+	23	123	150	5.1	.410	-3.0	C(27): -1.6	0.4
2016	ERI	AA	23	225	99	9.7	.351	0.5	C(56): 5.1	1.2
2017	ERI	AA	24	371	106	13.9	.266	-3.0	C(93): 27.5	3.8
2018	TOL	AAA	25	180	116	10.9	.336	0.3	C(44): 11.2	2.1
2018	DET	MLB	25	116	79	3.5	.313	0.3	C(30): -0.5	0.3
2019	DET	MLB	26	344	82	8.2	.287	-0.5	C 8	1.4

Grayson Greiner, continued

Batted Ball Distribution

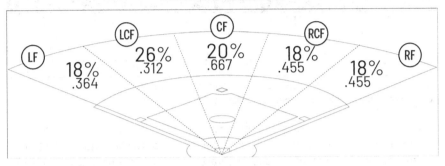

Strike Zone vs LHP   ## Strike Zone vs RHP

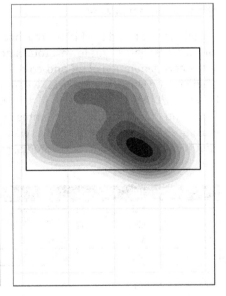

Josh Harrison INF

Born: 07/08/87   Age: 31   Bats: R   Throws: R
Height: 5'8"   Weight: 185   Origin: Round 6, 2008 Draft (#191 overall)

YEAR	TEAM	LVL	AGE	PA	R	2B	3B	HR	RBI	BB	K	SB	CS	AVG/OBP/SLG
2016	PIT	MLB	28	522	57	25	7	4	59	18	76	19	4	.283/.311/.388
2017	PIT	MLB	29	542	66	26	2	16	47	28	90	12	4	.272/.339/.432
2018	PIT	MLB	30	374	41	13	1	8	37	18	68	3	0	.250/.293/.363
2019	DET	MLB	31	462	57	22	3	10	43	25	80	10	3	.267/.326/.406

Breakout: 3%   Improve: 30%   Collapse: 10%   Attrition: 6%   MLB: 92%
Comparables: Omar Infante, Ronnie Belliard, Dutch Meyer

When Pittsburgh parted ways with Andrew McCutchen last winter, Harrison became the ersatz face of the franchise (albeit reluctantly; he requested a trade during Spring Training if the reloading Pirates weren't committed to winning in the short term). In some ways, Harrison is a more apt face of the franchise than Cutch was. A tough-as-nails player who isn't afraid to give up his body on both sides of the ball, Harrison has been a solid, if unspectacular, contributor outside of his career year in 2014.

Both Harrison and the Pirates reached a crossroads in 2018. He took the field for a mere 97 games, his lowest total since 2013, and the team took a long look at the next generation of up-and-coming Bucs in September. It has been a long, winding road since May 31, 2011, when Harrison debuted alongside a James McDonald/Dusty Brown battery in a lineup that included Lyle Overbay, Garrett Jones and Ronny Cedeno. The Pirates declined Harrison's $10.5 million option, making 2018 feel even more like a swan song, the torch handed gently to another generation of up-and-comers, much like Harrison when he made his Bucs debut.

YEAR	TEAM	LVL	AGE	PA	DRC+	VORP	BABIP	BRR	FRAA	WARP
2016	PIT	MLB	28	522	84	14.2	.323	3.1	2B(128): -0.1, RF(1): -0.2	0.8
2017	PIT	MLB	29	542	105	32.5	.303	1.7	2B(83): -2.6, 3B(49): 2.6	2.2
2018	PIT	MLB	30	374	87	3.0	.286	0.5	2B(87): -5.6, 3B(2): 0.0	0.0
2019	DET	MLB	31	462	101	17.4	.306	0.6	2B -2, 3B 0	1.4

Josh Harrison, continued

Batted Ball Distribution

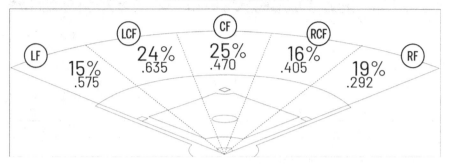

Strike Zone vs LHP   *Strike Zone vs RHP*

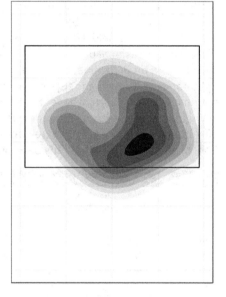

John Hicks 1B

Born: 08/31/89   Age: 29   Bats: R   Throws: R
Height: 6'2"   Weight: 230   Origin: Round 4, 2011 Draft (#123 overall)

YEAR	TEAM	LVL	AGE	PA	R	2B	3B	HR	RBI	BB	K	SB	CS	AVG/OBP/SLG
2016	ROC	AAA	26	34	1	2	0	1	1	1	5	0	0	.242/.265/.394
2016	ERI	AA	26	54	7	1	1	1	4	4	9	1	0	.388/.426/.510
2016	TOL	AAA	26	264	38	20	0	8	42	17	59	3	1	.303/.356/.485
2016	DET	MLB	26	2	1	1	0	0	0	0	0	0	0	.500/.500/1.000
2017	TOL	AAA	27	218	21	10	1	7	35	4	54	5	3	.269/.281/.428
2017	DET	MLB	27	190	25	12	0	6	22	13	51	2	1	.266/.326/.439
2018	DET	MLB	28	312	35	12	1	9	32	22	84	0	1	.260/.312/.403
2019	DET	MLB	29	395	40	18	2	11	44	24	102	3	2	.239/.289/.390

Breakout: 4%   Improve: 15%   Collapse: 13%   Attrition: 23%   MLB: 40%
Comparables: Ben Paulsen, Scott Thorman, Matt Downs

Find you a man who looks at you the way a manager looks at a third catcher. That's Hicks, versatile enough to catch a game, play first base and possibly corner outfield. He's a streaky player with occasional power and disappears a bit in the lineup when a

YEAR	TEAM	P. COUNT	FRM RUNS	BLK RUNS	THRW RUNS	TOT RUNS
2017	DET	2077	0.9	-0.1	0.0	1.2
2017	TOL	4951	2.8	0.5	0.0	3.6
2018	DET	2984	-0.9	-0.9	-0.1	-1.9
2019	DET	8618	-1.2	-0.3	0.0	-1.5

right-hander is throwing the sphere, which makes him better suited as the first option off the bench. He'll never be the best player from Goochland High School in Virginia, because Justin Verlander went there too, although Hicks did homer off Verlander in his first plate appearance. So, by transitive property, Goochland's field will eventually be Hicks Field.

YEAR	TEAM	LVL	AGE	PA	DRC+	VORP	BABIP	BRR	FRAA	WARP
2016	ROC	AAA	26	34	138	-0.3	.259	-0.1	C(9): -0.1	0.2
2016	ERI	AA	26	54	152	5.7	.450	0.4	C(11): 0.7, 1B(2): 0.2	0.6
2016	TOL	AAA	26	264	140	20.2	.374	-1.3	C(66): -1.1, 3B(1): 0.0	1.8
2016	DET	MLB	26	2	71	0.2	.500	-0.2	1B(1): 0.0	0.0
2017	TOL	AAA	27	218	85	5.8	.325	-0.5	C(37): 3.4, 1B(11): -0.8	0.2
2017	DET	MLB	27	190	80	1.1	.342	-1.0	1B(26): -0.4, C(18): 0.8	-0.1
2018	DET	MLB	28	312	91	1.8	.337	-1.3	1B(59): 0.3, C(21): -2.3	0.0
2019	DET	MLB	29	395	79	2.9	.299	-0.5	C -3, 1B -1	-0.2

John Hicks, continued

Batted Ball Distribution

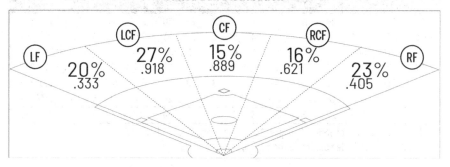

Strike Zone vs LHP   **Strike Zone vs RHP**

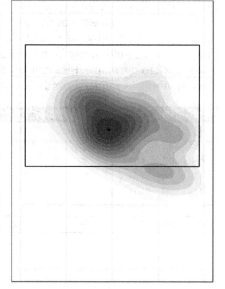

JaCoby Jones LF

Born: 05/10/92   Age: 27   Bats: R   Throws: R
Height: 6'2"   Weight: 201   Origin: Round 3, 2013 Draft (#87 overall)

YEAR	TEAM	LVL	AGE	PA	R	2B	3B	HR	RBI	BB	K	SB	CS	AVG/OBP/SLG
2016	ERI	AA	24	89	11	6	2	4	20	10	23	2	1	.312/.393/.597
2016	TOL	AAA	24	324	33	14	5	3	23	25	97	11	4	.243/.309/.356
2016	DET	MLB	24	28	3	3	0	0	2	0	12	0	0	.214/.214/.321
2017	TOL	AAA	25	393	57	19	2	9	44	33	104	12	4	.245/.314/.387
2017	DET	MLB	25	154	14	3	1	3	13	9	65	6	2	.170/.240/.270
2018	DET	MLB	26	467	54	22	6	11	34	24	142	13	5	.207/.266/.364
2019	DET	MLB	27	384	41	15	3	8	35	24	117	10	4	.208/.267/.336

Breakout: 6%   Improve: 36%   Collapse: 10%   Attrition: 20%   MLB: 77%
Comparables: Brian Anderson, Trayce Thompson, Laynce Nix

Jones still feels like a raw toolsy player, which isn't a positive quality for a 26-year-old. His rawness is mostly attributed to his hitting, which flashes occasional power with a strikeout percentage higher than his on-base percentage. His real value has been all things related to running fast. The zenith in his baserunning adventures came last September, when he scored from second base on a third-strike wild pitch. He remains a dangerous and smart runner, with plus-plus range in the outfield. He's exciting and athletic, but it all comes back to the maple. His inability to reach base is going to keep him from being anything beyond a second-division starter.

YEAR	TEAM	LVL	AGE	PA	DRC+	VORP	BABIP	BRR	FRAA	WARP
2016	ERI	AA	24	89	148	9.2	.392	-0.3	3B(9): -0.5, CF(9): 1.1	0.7
2016	TOL	AAA	24	324	87	6.9	.349	1.8	CF(57): -5.3, 3B(22): -1.3	-0.3
2016	DET	MLB	24	28	58	-1.2	.375	0.5	3B(6): 0.0, CF(5): -0.2	0.0
2017	TOL	AAA	25	393	92	15.9	.322	3.6	CF(76): 3.2, LF(7): 0.2	1.1
2017	DET	MLB	25	154	43	-8.0	.288	1.1	CF(51): 2.3, RF(1): 0.0	-0.2
2018	DET	MLB	26	467	67	-1.2	.281	4.3	CF(67): 4.0, LF(55): 2.7	0.7
2019	DET	MLB	27	384	67	2.2	.285	1.0	CF 3	0.2

JaCoby Jones, continued

Batted Ball Distribution

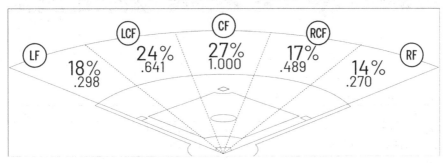

Strike Zone vs LHP

Strike Zone vs RHP

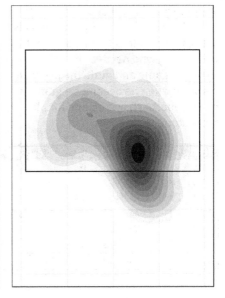

Dawel Lugo   2B

Born: 12/31/94   Age: 24   Bats: R   Throws: R
Height: 6'0"   Weight: 190   Origin: International Free Agent, 2012

YEAR	TEAM	LVL	AGE	PA	R	2B	3B	HR	RBI	BB	K	SB	CS	AVG/OBP/SLG
2016	VIS	A+	21	333	61	14	5	13	42	15	41	2	1	.314/.348/.514
2016	MOB	AA	21	177	24	9	2	4	20	4	15	1	1	.306/.322/.451
2017	WTN	AA	22	369	40	21	4	7	43	21	51	1	0	.282/.325/.428
2017	ERI	AA	22	188	18	6	1	6	22	12	21	2	1	.269/.314/.417
2018	TOL	AAA	23	523	56	26	3	3	59	9	66	12	4	.269/.283/.350
2018	DET	MLB	23	101	10	4	1	1	8	7	20	0	0	.213/.267/.309
2019	DET	MLB	24	232	21	10	1	5	22	4	37	1	1	.240/.254/.360

Breakout: 16%   Improve: 31%   Collapse: 2%   Attrition: 21%   MLB: 46%
Comparables: Scooter Gennett, Henry Rodriguez, Yangervis Solarte

The expectations and machinations of Lugo's batting approach should dictate better numbers, yes. He has a line-drive swing and it's yet to translate to any meaningful power. Baseball is a game of precision, where large moments occur at imprecise times. Lugo's first month of major-league action was swallowing him whole until he finally smacked his first home run in one of the wildest scenes for a 98-loss team: pinch-hitting in playoff atmosphere versus Milwaukee, who needed the game to contend for their division, off Josh Hader, to tie the game and mute the lively crowd. If that's the best he'll do, then that's his story when he becomes a grandfather. For now he needs to further refine his hitting approach and scrape for playing time at second base to accumulate more stories.

YEAR	TEAM	LVL	AGE	PA	DRC+	VORP	BABIP	BRR	FRAA	WARP
2016	VIS	A+	21	333	142	28.6	.328	2.5	3B(60): -3.5, SS(14): 2.0	1.8
2016	MOB	AA	21	177	122	13.3	.318	2.7	3B(41): 4.7, SS(10): 0.4	1.5
2017	WTN	AA	22	369	108	14.3	.310	-1.7	3B(77): 4.5, SS(10): -0.4	1.1
2017	ERI	AA	22	188	96	3.4	.275	-1.5	3B(29): -1.1, 2B(13): 0.6	-0.1
2018	TOL	AAA	23	523	82	1.8	.302	-1.1	2B(80): -6.0, 3B(43): -2.0	-1.1
2018	DET	MLB	23	101	77	-1.0	.260	-0.2	2B(27): -3.2	-0.3
2019	DET	MLB	24	232	58	-4.2	.264	-0.1	2B -3, 3B 0	-0.8

Dawel Lugo, continued

Batted Ball Distribution

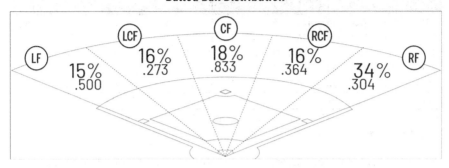

Strike Zone vs LHP   Strike Zone vs RHP

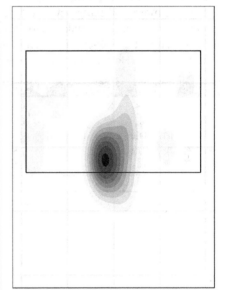

Mikie Mahtook   CF

Born: 11/30/89   Age: 29   Bats: R   Throws: R
Height: 6'1"   Weight: 216   Origin: Round 1, 2011 Draft (#31 overall)

YEAR	TEAM	LVL	AGE	PA	R	2B	3B	HR	RBI	BB	K	SB	CS	AVG/OBP/SLG
2016	DUR	AAA	26	120	16	5	3	1	7	12	24	5	1	.305/.383/.438
2016	TBA	MLB	26	196	16	9	0	3	11	7	68	0	1	.195/.231/.292
2017	DET	MLB	27	379	50	15	6	12	38	23	79	6	0	.276/.330/.457
2018	TOL	AAA	28	316	40	12	6	11	35	25	82	6	4	.251/.321/.452
2018	DET	MLB	28	250	24	4	2	9	29	21	66	4	1	.202/.276/.359
2019	DET	MLB	29	506	54	21	4	14	57	36	126	8	3	.237/.299/.391

Breakout: 5%   Improve: 27%   Collapse: 15%   Attrition: 23%   MLB: 68%
Comparables: Xavier Paul, Fred Lewis, Luis Terrero

Rebuilds are, at least for players, opportunities to show teams what they can do with enough playing time. Mahtook leveraged Detroit's hard reset in 2017, but in 2018 he was nearly invisible. For the first time since his rookie year he spent more time honing his swing in Triple-A than he did holding down an outfield spot in the majors. Missing out on a rebuild is like oversleeping for class; you're going to try to cram and make up for it but you're not going to retain much long term. As a result he's becoming a one-dimensional hitter, basically a few homers or nothing at all. He's a fourth outfielder at best, fifth in a non-rebuilding year.

YEAR	TEAM	LVL	AGE	PA	DRC+	VORP	BABIP	BRR	FRAA	WARP
2016	DUR	AAA	26	120	119	6.9	.383	0.6	CF(11): -1.1, RF(9): 1.9	0.5
2016	TBA	MLB	26	196	55	-11.6	.287	-1.2	LF(26): -0.9, CF(23): 0.5	-0.7
2017	DET	MLB	27	379	101	15.7	.324	1.6	CF(67): -1.6, RF(25): -1.7	1.0
2018	TOL	AAA	28	316	103	7.6	.313	-3.3	CF(36): 1.5, LF(24): 1.4	0.3
2018	DET	MLB	28	250	86	0.8	.238	0.5	LF(54): 6.9, RF(6): -1.2	0.8
2019	DET	MLB	29	506	90	8.0	.295	0.6	CF 0, RF -2	0.6

Mikie Mahtook, continued

Batted Ball Distribution

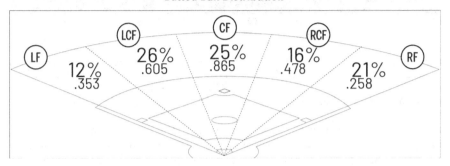

Strike Zone vs LHP   ### Strike Zone vs RHP

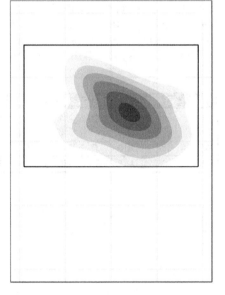

Jordy Mercer SS

Born: 08/27/86   Age: 32   Bats: R   Throws: R
Height: 6'3"   Weight: 210   Origin: Round 3, 2008 Draft (#79 overall)

YEAR	TEAM	LVL	AGE	PA	R	2B	3B	HR	RBI	BB	K	SB	CS	AVG/OBP/SLG
2016	PIT	MLB	29	584	66	22	3	11	59	51	83	1	1	.256/.328/.374
2017	PIT	MLB	30	558	52	24	5	14	58	51	88	0	4	.255/.326/.406
2018	PIT	MLB	31	436	43	29	2	6	39	32	87	2	0	.251/.315/.381
2019	DET	MLB	32	430	45	20	3	8	43	41	74	2	1	.255/.332/.386

Breakout: 2%   Improve: 32%   Collapse: 17%   Attrition: 17%   MLB: 95%
Comparables: Zack Cozart, Jack Wilson, Jason Bartlett

Appropriately, Mercer entered free agency this winter not with a bang but a whimper, sitting out most of September so the Pirates could get a long look at Kevin Newman. For the last three years Mercer was a cold streak away from losing his job, but somehow persevered despite subpar offense and defensive metrics that said he was pedestrian at best and outright bad/overmatched at shortstop at worst. While it's easy to point to how deep middle infield is now compared to 30 years ago, it still doesn't afford all 30 teams the ability to run a Francisco Lindor out there every day. We shouldn't wax poetically about Mercer's ordinariness, but surviving for six years as a major-league regular is worth something, even if that something is visible only under a magnifying glass.

YEAR	TEAM	LVL	AGE	PA	DRC+	VORP	BABIP	BRR	FRAA	WARP
2016	PIT	MLB	29	584	92	25.8	.286	3.0	SS(146): -7.4	1.6
2017	PIT	MLB	30	558	96	22.0	.284	-1.2	SS(144): -18.7	0.3
2018	PIT	MLB	31	436	87	10.6	.306	-1.0	SS(117): -3.0	0.9
2019	DET	MLB	32	430	97	16.2	.293	-0.7	SS -7	0.7

Jordy Mercer, continued

Batted Ball Distribution

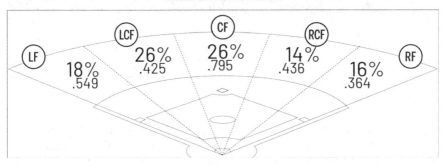

Strike Zone vs LHP   Strike Zone vs RHP

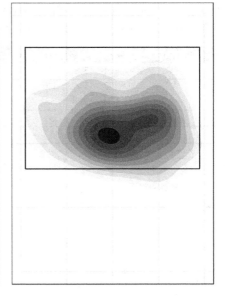

Victor Reyes LF

Born: 10/05/94   Age: 24   Bats: B   Throws: R
Height: 6'5"   Weight: 194   Origin: International Free Agent, 2011

YEAR	TEAM	LVL	AGE	PA	R	2B	3B	HR	RBI	BB	K	SB	CS	AVG/OBP/SLG
2016	VIS	A+	21	509	62	11	12	6	54	33	78	20	8	.303/.349/.416
2017	WTN	AA	22	516	59	29	5	4	51	27	80	18	9	.292/.332/.399
2018	DET	MLB	23	219	35	5	3	1	12	5	46	9	1	.222/.239/.288
2019	DET	MLB	24	344	36	13	3	6	30	20	71	10	3	.233/.283/.349

Breakout: 16%   Improve: 36%   Collapse: 1%   Attrition: 19%   MLB: 41%
Comparables: Raimel Tapia, Mitch Maier, Engel Beltre

It certainly wouldn't hurt Reyes to start the year in Triple-A after being woefully overmatched as a backup center fielder, but Rule 5 picks are almost destined to be overmatched if they stick in the majors all year. Among those with his playing time or better, he had the second-worst walk rate, the third-highest swing rate and the second-worst chase rate. Oddly enough — and perhaps there's a lesson in all this — he had 18 three-ball counts and never got a hit on any of them, though did reach base seven times and scored each time. For a free-swinging large dude, he has stunningly little power, so he'll rely on line drives and speed.

YEAR	TEAM	LVL	AGE	PA	DRC+	VORP	BABIP	BRR	FRAA	WARP
2016	VIS	A+	21	509	111	24.6	.352	1.3	RF(89): -7.0, LF(20): -2.6	-0.5
2017	WTN	AA	22	516	110	10.7	.342	0.1	RF(83): 4.9, CF(57): 10.8	2.5
2018	DET	MLB	23	219	63	-7.8	.277	0.1	LF(34): -3.2, CF(21): 2.2	-0.6
2019	DET	MLB	24	344	68	-3.6	.276	1.0	CF 2, LF -2	-0.3

Victor Reyes, continued

Batted Ball Distribution

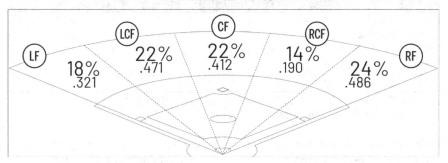

Strike Zone vs LHP   ## Strike Zone vs RHP

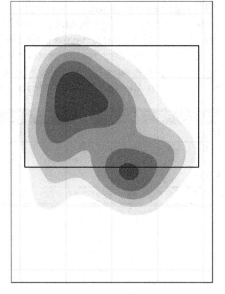

Ronny Rodriguez 2B

Born: 04/17/92   Age: 27   Bats: R   Throws: R
Height: 6'0"   Weight: 170   Origin: International Free Agent, 2010

YEAR	TEAM	LVL	AGE	PA	R	2B	3B	HR	RBI	BB	K	SB	CS	AVG/OBP/SLG
2016	COH	AAA	24	488	58	24	5	10	59	22	88	4	4	.258/.293/.400
2017	COH	AAA	25	483	60	18	2	17	64	23	92	15	5	.291/.324/.454
2018	TOL	AAA	26	275	42	20	5	9	40	10	47	10	8	.338/.365/.558
2018	DET	MLB	26	206	17	7	0	5	20	10	42	2	0	.220/.256/.335
2019	DET	MLB	27	228	24	9	2	7	26	8	49	4	2	.247/.274/.405

Breakout: 8%   Improve: 31%   Collapse: 10%   Attrition: 34%   MLB: 65%
Comparables: Tyler Greene, Elliot Johnson, Phil Gosselin

After 800 games as a minor leaguer followed by minor-league free agency, the toolsy Rodriguez finally reached the bigs, at which point his peculiar bat wielding — holding the bat vertical for a while, then parallel completely above his head — resulted in the Batting Stance Guy treatment. A midseason slump resulted in hitting coach Lloyd McClendon cleaning up the approach and ditching the idiosyncrasies, not unlike Wilson in *Cast Away*. He's an average hitter with double-digit-homer potential and can play anywhere, including shortstop, so he'll likely have a major-league job for now. But if things ever turn south, he can fall back on his winter gig: musician. As "El Felino," his YouTube record page has over 19,000 subscribers, with one song reaching 300,000 views, which is more than he'll ever get for his now-mundane but solid stance.

YEAR	TEAM	LVL	AGE	PA	DRC+	VORP	BABIP	BRR	FRAA	WARP
2016	COH	AAA	24	488	89	8.4	.298	-0.2	2B(85): 1.4, 1B(17): 0.4	0.4
2017	COH	AAA	25	483	106	11.5	.329	-1.4	2B(62): 7.9, 3B(25): 1.6	2.5
2018	TOL	AAA	26	275	156	30.8	.383	-1.8	3B(34): 2.1, SS(26): -0.9	2.3
2018	DET	MLB	26	206	77	-4.3	.253	-0.3	SS(24): -2.3, 2B(17): 0.1	-0.3
2019	DET	MLB	27	228	78	0.7	.279	0.1	SS 0, 1B 0	0.1

Ronny Rodriguez, continued

Batted Ball Distribution

Strike Zone vs LHP   Strike Zone vs RHP

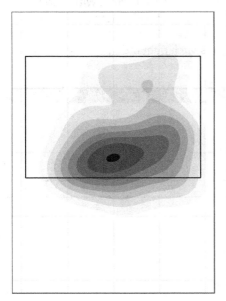 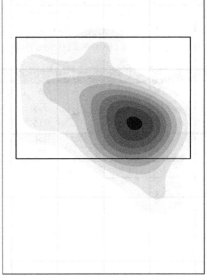

Christin Stewart LF

Born: 12/10/93   Age: 25   Bats: L   Throws: R
Height: 6'0"   Weight: 205   Origin: Round 1, 2015 Draft (#34 overall)

YEAR	TEAM	LVL	AGE	PA	R	2B	3B	HR	RBI	BB	K	SB	CS	AVG/OBP/SLG
2016	LAK	A+	22	442	60	22	1	24	68	74	105	3	1	.264/.403/.534
2016	ERI	AA	22	100	17	2	0	6	19	12	26	0	0	.218/.310/.448
2017	ERI	AA	23	555	67	29	3	28	86	56	138	3	0	.256/.335/.501
2018	TOL	AAA	24	522	69	21	3	23	77	67	108	0	0	.264/.364/.480
2018	DET	MLB	24	72	7	1	1	2	10	10	13	0	0	.267/.375/.417
2019	DET	MLB	25	486	55	16	2	21	64	44	125	0	0	.207/.284/.399

Breakout: 14%   Improve: 44%   Collapse: 4%   Attrition: 33%   MLB: 73%
Comparables: Khris Davis, Jerry Sands, Matt LaPorta

Service-time manipulation be damned, the rebuilding Tigers did the unthinkable in a non-cost-saving move and gave their three-time minor-league player of the year the left field job for a month. The tryout checked all the boxes and Stewart is on the inside track to start the season in Detroit. With a homer every 20 minor-league plate appearances, his power will dictate his usefulness, since a young dude in left field is fine for now, but long term he's looking at 1B/DH. In fact, he'll probably be ready for that switch right around the time when Miguel Cabrera's contract strikes midnight.

YEAR	TEAM	LVL	AGE	PA	DRC+	VORP	BABIP	BRR	FRAA	WARP
2016	LAK	A+	22	442	169	32.4	.306	-6.6	LF(94): -15.2	0.8
2016	ERI	AA	22	100	128	4.1	.232	0.7	LF(22): 1.0	0.5
2017	ERI	AA	23	555	116	31.3	.294	-0.8	LF(124): -10.6	-0.1
2018	TOL	AAA	24	522	136	36.1	.296	0.8	LF(97): 9.8, RF(12): -0.7	3.5
2018	DET	MLB	24	72	107	3.4	.304	-0.3	LF(15): -0.9	0.1
2019	DET	MLB	25	486	88	7.6	.236	-0.7	LF 0	0.6

Christin Stewart, continued

Batted Ball Distribution

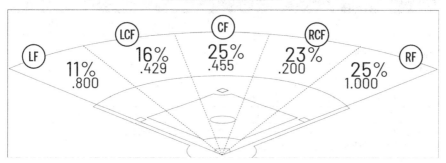

Strike Zone vs LHP

Strike Zone vs RHP

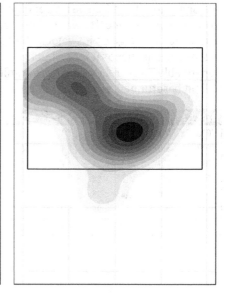

Victor Alcantara   RHP

Born: 04/03/93   Age: 26   Bats: R   Throws: R
Height: 6'2"   Weight: 190   Origin: International Free Agent, 2011

YEAR	TEAM	LVL	AGE	W	L	SV	G	GS	IP	H	HR	BB/9	K/9	K	GB%	BABIP
2016	ARK	AA	23	3	7	0	29	20	111	106	9	4.6	6.4	79	55%	.289
2017	ERI	AA	24	1	2	1	30	2	54²	46	1	5.6	9.4	57	60%	.312
2017	TOL	AAA	24	0	1	0	9	1	20	22	0	5.4	7.2	16	54%	.338
2017	DET	MLB	24	0	0	0	6	0	7¹	12	1	4.9	6.1	5	54%	.407
2018	TOL	AAA	25	5	2	3	29	1	51¹	52	3	1.2	8.2	47	55%	.329
2018	DET	MLB	25	1	1	0	27	0	30	25	5	1.8	6.3	21	51%	.230
2019	DET	MLB	26	2	3	0	48	0	51	49	5	3.9	7.9	45	50%	.295

Breakout: 20%   Improve: 34%   Collapse: 10%   Attrition: 21%   MLB: 53%
Comparables: Joely Rodriguez, Zach Phillips, Donn Roach

"If he can figure out his control, he'll be a good pitcher" is the "thoughts and prayers" of relievers. Alcantara, the raw-power, salary-dump return for Cameron Maybin, struggled with command throughout his minor-league career, averaging about five free bases per nine innings at each rung. Last year, he cut it to below two per nine. He was still prone to allowing gopher balls and other hard contact, and given his velocity he has surprising trouble getting swings and misses when he needs it most, but his breakout year made him one of the most dependable Tigers relievers. That's admittedly a low bar, but his sudden ability to limit baserunners would make him a good late option for any team.

YEAR	TEAM	LVL	AGE	WHIP	ERA	DRA	WARP	MPH	FB%	WHF	CSP
2016	ARK	AA	23	1.47	4.30	3.74	1.7				
2017	ERI	AA	24	1.46	3.46	3.97	0.6				
2017	TOL	AAA	24	1.70	4.05	4.10	0.3				
2017	DET	MLB	24	2.18	8.59	5.22	0.0	94.6	76.1	12.7	45.3
2018	TOL	AAA	25	1.15	2.81	3.06	1.2				
2018	DET	MLB	25	1.03	2.40	4.35	0.2	95.2	72.5	10.9	48.5
2019	DET	MLB	26	1.40	4.30	4.56	0.3	94.7	74.5	11.5	47.9

Victor Alcantara, continued

Pitch Shape vs LHH   ### Pitch Shape vs RHH

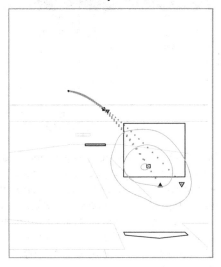

Type	Frequency	Velocity	H Movement	V Movement
● Fastball	1.6%	94.8 [107]	-10.7 [81]	-16.1 [99]
□ Sinker	70.9%	94.1 [108]	-14 [89]	-21.2 [97]
+ Cutter				
▲ Changeup	18.6%	88.4 [112]	-13.2 [90]	-24.6 [108]
✕ Splitter				
▽ Slider	8.9%	90.2 [126]	-3.3 [65]	-23.4 [128]
◇ Curveball				
✥ Slow Curveball				
✳ Knuckleball				
▼ Screwball				

Sandy Baez   RHP

Born: 11/25/93   Age: 25   Bats: R   Throws: R
Height: 6'2"   Weight: 180   Origin: International Free Agent, 2011

YEAR	TEAM	LVL	AGE	W	L	SV	G	GS	IP	H	HR	BB/9	K/9	K	GB%	BABIP
2016	WMI	A	22	7	9	0	21	21	113¹	125	7	2.2	7.0	88	40%	.337
2017	LAK	A+	23	6	7	0	17	17	88²	88	7	2.4	9.3	92	39%	.328
2017	ERI	AA	23	0	1	0	2	2	10	9	3	4.5	11.7	13	36%	.273
2018	ERI	AA	24	1	9	1	33	15	103²	114	19	4.0	7.5	86	38%	.316
2018	DET	MLB	24	0	0	0	9	0	14¹	12	2	5.7	6.3	10	31%	.233
2019	DET	MLB	25	2	3	0	54	0	56	59	8	3.7	7.4	47	36%	.297

Breakout: 0%   Improve: 1%   Collapse: 0%   Attrition: 2%   MLB: 2%
Comparables: Angel Sanchez, Francisco Cruceta, Sam LeCure

Double-A was not kind to Baez, who was kindly asked to leave the rotation. However, existing on the 40-man roster of a team desperate for men with velocity allowed him to poke his head up as the 26th man for a doubleheader, no-hitting the Yankees over 4 1/3 innings in a mop-up appearance. His September sequel was less successful, and hitting his spots wasn't any easier under the bright lights. The closest Baez will be to becoming a successful reliever is being an anagram of Danys Baez, which is more than you can say for most struggling pitchers.

YEAR	TEAM	LVL	AGE	WHIP	ERA	DRA	WARP	MPH	FB%	WHF	CSP
2016	WMI	A	22	1.35	3.81	3.71	1.8				
2017	LAK	A+	23	1.26	3.86	3.32	2.0				
2017	ERI	AA	23	1.40	4.50	3.30	0.2				
2018	ERI	AA	24	1.54	5.64	4.78	0.6				
2018	DET	MLB	24	1.47	5.02	6.65	-0.3	97.8	63.7	8.5	46.8
2019	DET	MLB	25	1.45	5.11	5.18	0.0	97.5	65.2	8.7	48

Sandy Baez, continued

Pitch Shape vs LHH

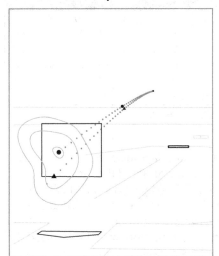

Pitch Shape vs RHH

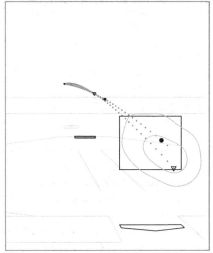

Type	Frequency	Velocity	H Movement	V Movement
● Fastball	63.3%	95.4 [109]	-8.5 [92]	-13.9 [106]
□ Sinker	0.4%	84.5 [60]	-9.2 [128]	-25 [85]
+ Cutter				
▲ Changeup	14.1%	86.7 [106]	-9.2 [111]	-23.7 [111]
✕ Splitter				
▽ Slider	20.7%	81.8 [88]	4.6 [99]	-34.4 [96]
◇ Curveball	1.5%	76.9 [94]	7.5 [99]	-43.1 [111]
✦ Slow Curveball				
✱ Knuckleball				
▼ Screwball				

Matt Boyd   LHP

Born: 02/02/91   Age: 28   Bats: L   Throws: L
Height: 6'3"   Weight: 234   Origin: Round 6, 2013 Draft (#175 overall)

YEAR	TEAM	LVL	AGE	W	L	SV	G	GS	IP	H	HR	BB/9	K/9	K	GB%	BABIP
2016	TOL	AAA	25	2	5	0	11	11	64	53	5	2.5	8.0	57	42%	.271
2016	DET	MLB	25	6	5	0	20	18	97¹	97	17	2.7	7.6	82	39%	.286
2017	TOL	AAA	26	3	3	0	8	8	51	35	7	2.3	9.4	53	39%	.224
2017	DET	MLB	26	6	11	0	26	25	135	157	18	3.5	7.3	110	40%	.330
2018	DET	MLB	27	9	13	0	31	31	170¹	146	27	2.7	8.4	159	30%	.258
2019	DET	MLB	28	8	12	0	28	28	159	159	27	2.9	8.0	142	36%	.289

Breakout: 25%   Improve: 58%   Collapse: 10%   Attrition: 19%   MLB: 88%
Comparables: Chris Young, Zach McAllister, John Maine

When astronaut Scott Kelly spent 340 consecutive days in space — the longest such stint in the International Space Station — it's rumored that he finally wanted to come home because he was tired of finding Boyd's curveballs and changeups. When he takes the mound, birds are mobilized and asked to stay in their nests for security reasons. The United Nations routinely asks Boyd to throw bullpen sessions in areas of the world suffering from drought so he can seed the clouds. He's sort of a fly-ball pitcher, is what we're saying. Aerial assaults aside, Boyd still tosses a variety of pitches and is developing into an innings eater with a very average ERA. Expect anything more from him and your head is up in the clouds, which as mentioned, is the worst place to be when Boyd pitches.

YEAR	TEAM	LVL	AGE	WHIP	ERA	DRA	WARP	MPH	FB%	WHF	CSP
2016	TOL	AAA	25	1.11	2.25	3.34	1.5				
2016	DET	MLB	25	1.29	4.53	5.94	-0.7	94.3	60.9	10.2	49.2
2017	TOL	AAA	26	0.94	2.82	3.53	1.2				
2017	DET	MLB	26	1.56	5.27	6.46	-1.3	94.3	50.7	11	48
2018	DET	MLB	27	1.16	4.39	5.22	0.2	93.5	48.9	10.9	49
2019	DET	MLB	28	1.32	4.70	5.09	0.6	93.3	51.9	10.9	49

Matt Boyd, continued

Pitch Shape vs LHH

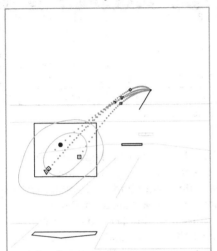

Pitch Shape vs RHH

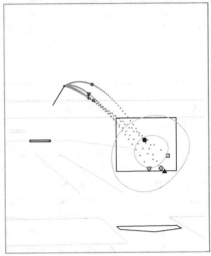

Type	Frequency	Velocity	H Movement	V Movement
● Fastball	38.8%	91.1 [96]	8.7 [91]	-16 [99]
□ Sinker	10.0%	89.7 [86]	13.6 [92]	-20.5 [100]
+ Cutter				
▲ Changeup	7.7%	78.9 [74]	9.8 [108]	-30.2 [92]
✕ Splitter				
▽ Slider	31.1%	81 [84]	-1.5 [85]	-35.4 [93]
◇ Curveball	12.3%	72.6 [78]	-11.8 [117]	-50 [96]
⊕ Slow Curveball				
✱ Knuckleball				
▼ Screwball				

Louis Coleman RHP

Born: 04/04/86   Age: 33   Bats: R   Throws: R
Height: 6'4"   Weight: 205   Origin: Round 5, 2009 Draft (#152 overall)

YEAR	TEAM	LVL	AGE	W	L	SV	G	GS	IP	H	HR	BB/9	K/9	K	GB%	BABIP
2016	LAN	MLB	30	2	1	0	61	0	48	45	5	4.5	8.4	45	37%	.299
2017	LOU	AAA	31	2	1	2	25	0	36²	28	1	3.9	10.8	44	33%	.303
2017	RNO	AAA	31	2	1	0	25	0	27¹	16	2	5.3	10.9	33	35%	.230
2018	TOL	AAA	32	0	0	8	13	0	15	8	1	3.0	9.0	15	43%	.194
2018	DET	MLB	32	4	1	0	51	0	51¹	43	5	4.2	7.2	41	44%	.270
2019	DET	MLB	33	1	1	0	21	0	22²	22	3	4.5	7.7	19	40%	.290

Breakout: 18%   Improve: 24%   Collapse: 19%   Attrition: 18%   MLB: 48%
Comparables: Tommy Layne, Jean Machi, Dale Thayer

Coleman's sidearm-ish right-handed delivery has historically kept same-sided hitters silent. However, last year, in his first extended MLB playing time in a while, his platoon splits went tail over teakettle. Right-handers sat on his fastball while left-handers were thrown off balance with a new changeup. But no manager is going to call on him to retire lefties; he'll simply need to better hide that four-seamer so he can return to his specialty. Even if that happens, Coleman's command has always been too suspect to use him in high-leverage situations. He provides solid bullpen depth with a different look, and that's about it.

YEAR	TEAM	LVL	AGE	WHIP	ERA	DRA	WARP	MPH	FB%	WHF	CSP
2016	LAN	MLB	30	1.44	4.69	4.05	0.5	91.9	39.5	12.9	40.9
2017	LOU	AAA	31	1.20	2.21	3.90	0.6				
2017	RNO	AAA	31	1.17	2.30	4.05	0.4				
2018	TOL	AAA	32	0.87	2.40	2.41	0.5				
2018	DET	MLB	32	1.31	3.51	5.30	-0.2	91.2	54.3	12	40.5
2019	DET	MLB	33	1.46	5.17	5.22	0.0	90.4	48	12.2	40.2

Louis Coleman, continued

Pitch Shape vs LHH

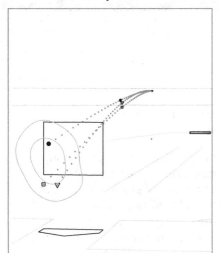

Pitch Shape vs RHH

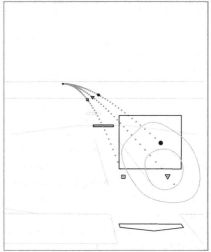

Type		Frequency	Velocity	H Movement	V Movement
●	Fastball	39.9%	90.1 [92]	-7.6 [96]	-19 [90]
□	Sinker	14.4%	88.2 [79]	-11.8 [107]	-30.6 [66]
+	Cutter				
▲	Changeup	0.5%	85.4 [100]	-12.4 [94]	-32.6 [84]
✕	Splitter				
▽	Slider	45.0%	83.3 [95]	4.8 [100]	-34.2 [97]
◇	Curveball	0.2%	73.2 [81]	6.9 [96]	-52.6 [90]
✦	Slow Curveball				
✳	Knuckleball				
▼	Screwball				

Buck Farmer RHP

Born: 02/20/91   Age: 28   Bats: L   Throws: R
Height: 6'4"   Weight: 232   Origin: Round 5, 2013 Draft (#156 overall)

YEAR	TEAM	LVL	AGE	W	L	SV	G	GS	IP	H	HR	BB/9	K/9	K	GB%	BABIP
2016	TOL	AAA	25	5	6	0	20	20	100	106	11	2.5	8.4	93	47%	.326
2016	DET	MLB	25	0	1	0	14	1	29^1	25	4	6.1	8.3	27	52%	.266
2017	TOL	AAA	26	6	4	0	21	21	123^2	133	9	2.3	8.3	114	43%	.343
2017	DET	MLB	26	5	5	0	11	11	48	55	9	3.8	9.2	49	34%	.336
2018	DET	MLB	27	3	4	0	66	1	69^1	67	6	5.3	7.4	57	41%	.300
2019	DET	MLB	28	2	3	0	48	0	51	51	6	3.9	8.1	46	42%	.298

Breakout: 30%   Improve: 54%   Collapse: 16%   Attrition: 23%   MLB: 81%
Comparables: Dan Meyer, Craig Stammen, Shane Greene

Every good agricultural expert knows not to give out too many free samples, yet Farmer led last year's Tigers bullpen in free passes. Scarecrow malfunctions aside, his fastball-changeup combination kept the sphere in the park, even if that park was the cavernous Comerica. He might still have premonitions of being in the rotation someday, but relievers with two solid yet wild pitches are prone to travel from parcel to parcel, collecting several different souvenir uniforms along the way.

YEAR	TEAM	LVL	AGE	WHIP	ERA	DRA	WARP	MPH	FB%	WHF	CSP
2016	TOL	AAA	25	1.34	3.96	2.97	2.7				
2016	DET	MLB	25	1.53	4.60	4.78	0.1	95.5	61.4	11.5	41.4
2017	TOL	AAA	26	1.33	3.93	3.79	2.6				
2017	DET	MLB	26	1.56	6.75	5.85	-0.1	93.9	61.2	11.7	45.7
2018	DET	MLB	27	1.56	4.15	5.49	-0.4	96.0	57.6	12	45.3
2019	DET	MLB	28	1.42	4.45	4.68	0.3	94.7	59.6	11.9	44.7

Buck Farmer, continued

Pitch Shape vs LHH

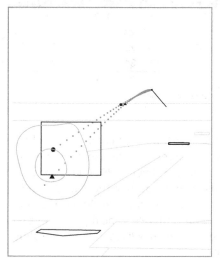

Pitch Shape vs RHH

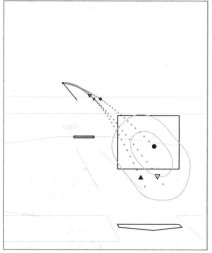

Type		Frequency	Velocity	H Movement	V Movement
●	Fastball	57.4%	95 [108]	-10.8 [81]	-14.7 [103]
□	Sinker	0.2%	92.3 [99]	-15.3 [78]	-23.7 [89]
+	Cutter				
▲	Changeup	25.2%	87.3 [108]	-14.1 [85]	-32.7 [84]
×	Splitter				
▽	Slider	17.3%	81.3 [86]	2.2 [89]	-35.1 [94]
◇	Curveball				
⬦	Slow Curveball				
✳	Knuckleball				
▼	Screwball				

Michael Fulmer RHP

Born: 03/15/93 Age: 26 Bats: R Throws: R
Height: 6'3" Weight: 246 Origin: Round 1, 2011 Draft (#44 overall)

YEAR	TEAM	LVL	AGE	W	L	SV	G	GS	IP	H	HR	BB/9	K/9	K	GB%	BABIP
2016	TOL	AAA	23	1	1	0	3	3	15¹	16	3	2.9	11.7	20	49%	.325
2016	DET	MLB	23	11	7	0	26	26	159	136	16	2.4	7.5	132	51%	.268
2017	DET	MLB	24	10	12	0	25	25	164²	150	13	2.2	6.2	114	51%	.273
2018	DET	MLB	25	3	12	0	24	24	132¹	128	19	3.1	7.5	110	47%	.288
2019	DET	MLB	26	6	8	0	21	21	119²	115	13	2.8	7.5	100	47%	.290

Breakout: 21% Improve: 60% Collapse: 22% Attrition: 9% MLB: 93%
Comparables: Sonny Gray, Marcus Stroman, Jesse Hahn

Fulmer was able to avoid the sophomore slump, but the junior jinx was right on schedule. He had two disabled list stints for different non-arm injuries, which never help, but he also tinkered with his signature slider. In 2017 it was one of the hardest-thrown sliders in baseball. Last year he brought the velocity down on purpose and added some more sweeping action, and it resulted in the ball flying out the park far too often. Needless to say, there's some figuring out to do with respect to his devastating breaking pitch, which will result in "senior slider" having either the good or bad connotation.

YEAR	TEAM	LVL	AGE	WHIP	ERA	DRA	WARP	MPH	FB%	WHF	CSP
2016	TOL	AAA	23	1.37	4.11	3.22	0.4				
2016	DET	MLB	23	1.12	3.06	4.30	1.9	97.3	56.8	11.5	45.8
2017	DET	MLB	24	1.15	3.83	3.75	3.4	97.7	59.4	10.5	48.6
2018	DET	MLB	25	1.31	4.69	4.66	1.0	97.8	61	11.7	48.6
2019	DET	MLB	26	1.26	3.94	4.26	1.6	97.2	60.4	11.4	48.7

Michael Fulmer, continued

Pitch Shape vs LHH

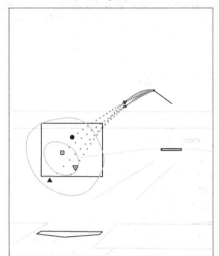

Pitch Shape vs RHH

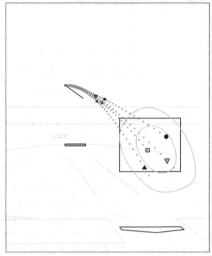

Type	Frequency	Velocity	H Movement	V Movement
● Fastball	25.5%	96.5 [113]	-2.4 [120]	-11.9 [112]
□ Sinker	35.5%	96.3 [119]	-12.1 [104]	-16 [114]
+ Cutter				
▲ Changeup	14.3%	88.5 [113]	-10.5 [104]	-27.7 [99]
✕ Splitter				
▽ Slider	24.8%	86.7 [110]	7.5 [111]	-31.4 [105]
◇ Curveball				
⊕ Slow Curveball				
✳ Knuckleball				
▼ Screwball				

Shane Greene   RHP

Born: 11/17/88   Age: 30   Bats: R   Throws: R
Height: 6'4"   Weight: 197   Origin: Round 15, 2009 Draft (#465 overall)

YEAR	TEAM	LVL	AGE	W	L	SV	G	GS	IP	H	HR	BB/9	K/9	K	GB%	BABIP
2016	DET	MLB	27	5	4	2	50	3	60¹	58	3	3.3	8.8	59	48%	.327
2017	DET	MLB	28	4	3	9	71	0	67²	50	6	4.5	9.7	73	49%	.265
2018	DET	MLB	29	4	6	32	66	0	63¹	68	12	2.7	9.2	65	42%	.311
2019	DET	MLB	30	2	3	21	54	0	56	53	6	3.5	8.7	55	44%	.301

Breakout: 18%   Improve: 50%   Collapse: 15%   Attrition: 11%   MLB: 80%
Comparables: Brian Matusz, Tom Gorzelanny, Trevor Cahill

In *Monsters University*, the plucky one-eyed green critter Mike Wazowski was well-read in the technical side of scaring but ultimately could not convince Dean Hardscrabble of his scaring ability for the simple fact that he just wasn't scary. Likewise, Greene has a closer's mentality but not a closer's stuff. As a result, he *is* scary with a tight lead. For a team way out of contention, he was used surprisingly often, twice pitching on four consecutive days and once in both ends of a double-header. The fatigue showed, especially at the end of the season, and taters were his undoing. He's embraced high-leverage situations but would be best used sparingly, probably not as a closer. However, a manager can rely on him to enter a game to strand some baserunners and put some rallies right to bed with nightmares.

YEAR	TEAM	LVL	AGE	WHIP	ERA	DRA	WARP	MPH	FB%	WHF	CSP
2016	DET	MLB	27	1.33	5.82	4.20	0.6	96.2	40.8	13.7	46.3
2017	DET	MLB	28	1.24	2.66	4.56	0.5	96.4	56.2	9.8	52
2018	DET	MLB	29	1.37	5.12	3.94	0.7	95.9	50.8	9.9	51.1
2019	DET	MLB	30	1.35	3.78	4.13	0.7	95.4	50.2	10.7	50.1

Shane Greene, continued

Pitch Shape vs LHH

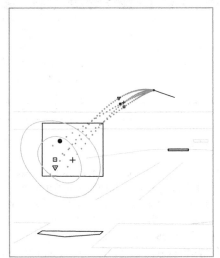

Pitch Shape vs RHH

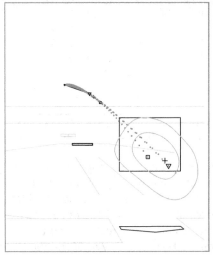

Type	Frequency	Velocity	H Movement	V Movement
● Fastball	5.7%	95.5 [109]	-5.5 [105]	-12.9 [109]
□ Sinker	45.1%	94.6 [111]	-13.1 [96]	-18.1 [107]
+ Cutter	24.0%	88.6 [99]	6.9 [129]	-25.9 [91]
▲ Changeup				
✕ Splitter				
▽ Slider	25.2%	81.6 [87]	14.2 [141]	-35.2 [93]
◇ Curveball				
⊕ Slow Curveball				
✱ Knuckleball				
▼ Screwball				

Blaine Hardy LHP

Born: 03/14/87 Age: 32 Bats: L Throws: L
Height: 6'2" Weight: 218 Origin: Round 22, 2008 Draft (#655 overall)

YEAR	TEAM	LVL	AGE	W	L	SV	G	GS	IP	H	HR	BB/9	K/9	K	GB%	BABIP
2016	TOL	AAA	29	1	0	1	32	0	31^1	20	1	1.4	5.5	19	56%	.213
2016	DET	MLB	29	1	0	0	21	0	25^2	25	2	4.2	7.0	20	49%	.295
2017	TOL	AAA	30	7	3	3	34	2	40^2	32	1	1.1	10.0	45	48%	.304
2017	DET	MLB	30	1	0	0	35	0	33^1	46	7	3.5	7.6	28	34%	.361
2018	TOL	AAA	31	3	0	0	9	4	26^1	14	0	1.4	11.6	34	39%	.250
2018	DET	MLB	31	4	5	1	30	13	86	79	10	2.3	6.9	66	42%	.275
2019	DET	MLB	32	3	4	0	37	5	59	61	9	3.2	7.5	49	44%	.295

Breakout: 20% Improve: 35% Collapse: 28% Attrition: 15% MLB: 75%
Comparables: Anthony Varvaro, Cesar Ramos, Brandon Kintzler

After 164 big-league appearances — all in relief — the veteran lefty reinvigorated his career in 2018 by stretching out in the rotation, proving himself in Triple-A and then posting the second-best ERA by a Tigers starter. Hardy averaged about five innings per start and once took a no-hitter into the seventh, but was drastically more effective in his traditional role (0.98 ERA, in 18 1/3 innings of relief). He barely throws 90, but he's a lefty with control, a stellar curveball and newly discovered stamina. Those are all career-extending qualities. Platoon him with Yusmeiro Petit and send the rest of your bullpen home for the night.

YEAR	TEAM	LVL	AGE	WHIP	ERA	DRA	WARP	MPH	FB%	WHF	CSP
2016	TOL	AAA	29	0.80	1.72	3.08	0.7				
2016	DET	MLB	29	1.44	3.51	4.99	0.0	91.1	49.2	10.5	47.4
2017	TOL	AAA	30	0.91	3.10	1.77	1.6				
2017	DET	MLB	30	1.77	5.94	5.24	0.0	91.3	44.9	11.3	49.8
2018	TOL	AAA	31	0.68	1.03	2.40	0.9				
2018	DET	MLB	31	1.17	3.56	3.98	1.2	90.2	32.9	9.1	51.5
2019	DET	MLB	32	1.40	4.82	5.02	0.2	89.6	37.3	9.7	49.4

Blaine Hardy, continued

Pitch Shape vs LHH	Pitch Shape vs RHH
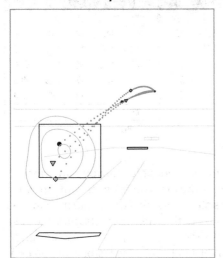	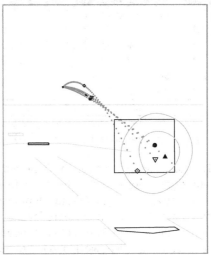

Type	Frequency	Velocity	H Movement	V Movement
● Fastball	31.5%	88.3 [87]	5.3 [106]	-14.7 [103]
□ Sinker	1.4%	89.2 [84]	12.2 [103]	-18.4 [106]
+ Cutter				
▲ Changeup	24.1%	80 [79]	15.1 [79]	-28.7 [96]
✕ Splitter				
▽ Slider	33.8%	84 [98]	-3.7 [95]	-27.2 [117]
◇ Curveball	9.2%	75.8 [90]	-4.3 [85]	-56.5 [81]
⊕ Slow Curveball				
✱ Knuckleball				
▼ Screwball				

Joe Jimenez RHP

Born: 01/17/95   Age: 24   Bats: R   Throws: R
Height: 6'3"   Weight: 272   Origin: Undrafted Free Agent, 2013

YEAR	TEAM	LVL	AGE	W	L	SV	G	GS	IP	H	HR	BB/9	K/9	K	GB%	BABIP
2016	LAK	A+	21	0	0	10	17	0	17¹	5	0	2.6	14.5	28	36%	.179
2016	ERI	AA	21	3	2	12	21	0	20²	12	0	3.5	14.8	34	24%	.316
2016	TOL	AAA	21	0	1	8	17	0	15²	9	1	2.3	9.2	16	38%	.205
2017	TOL	AAA	22	1	1	4	26	0	25	19	1	4.3	13.0	36	43%	.340
2017	DET	MLB	22	0	2	0	24	0	19	31	4	4.3	8.1	17	37%	.403
2018	DET	MLB	23	5	4	3	68	0	62²	53	5	3.2	11.2	78	36%	.304
2019	DET	MLB	24	3	3	12	59	0	62	56	8	3.9	10.4	72	37%	.298

Breakout: 26%   Improve: 38%   Collapse: 24%   Attrition: 25%   MLB: 80%
Comparables: Corey Knebel, Josh Spence, Keone Kela

They said it couldn't happen. They said it was impossible. But you remember where you were — hopefully sitting down — the moment a Tigers homegrown reliever was named an All-Star. Jimenez's strong first half as a setup man made him Detroit's first non-closer reliever named to the Midseason Classic since Mike Henneman in 1989. The explosive fastball-slider two-step generates whiffs and weak contact. A high workload led to diminishing zip on the fastball and an ERA on the wrong side of seven for the last two months, because did we mention he was a Tigers reliever? Sometimes impossibility is mistaken for inevitability. However, Jimenez showed the work ethic and the results, and the 24-year-old will eventually be the ninth-inning stopper.

YEAR	TEAM	LVL	AGE	WHIP	ERA	DRA	WARP	MPH	FB%	WHF	CSP
2016	LAK	A+	21	0.58	0.00	2.11	0.6				
2016	ERI	AA	21	0.97	2.18	1.86	0.7				
2016	TOL	AAA	21	0.83	2.30	2.53	0.4				
2017	TOL	AAA	22	1.24	1.44	2.37	0.8				
2017	DET	MLB	22	2.11	12.32	5.25	0.0	97.2	63.1	12.8	52
2018	DET	MLB	23	1.20	4.31	3.05	1.4	97.6	67.2	14.7	47.3
2019	DET	MLB	24	1.32	3.79	4.13	0.7	97.3	68.3	14.7	50.9

Joe Jimenez, continued

Pitch Shape vs LHH

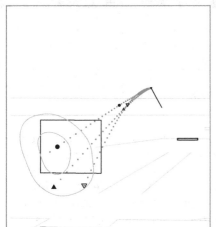

Pitch Shape vs RHH

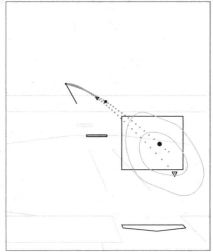

Type	Frequency	Velocity	H Movement	V Movement
● Fastball	67.2%	96.1 [112]	-9 [89]	-11.5 [113]
☐ Sinker				
+ Cutter				
▲ Changeup	10.8%	89.8 [118]	-12 [96]	-26.9 [101]
✕ Splitter				
▽ Slider	22.0%	85.9 [106]	6.3 [106]	-30.6 [107]
◇ Curveball				
⊕ Slow Curveball				
✳ Knuckleball				
▼ Screwball				

Matt Moore LHP

Born: 06/18/89   Age: 30   Bats: L   Throws: L
Height: 6'3"   Weight: 210   Origin: Round 8, 2007 Draft (#245 overall)

YEAR	TEAM	LVL	AGE	W	L	SV	G	GS	IP	H	HR	BB/9	K/9	K	GB%	BABIP
2016	TBA	MLB	27	7	7	0	21	21	130	125	20	2.8	7.5	109	38%	.280
2016	SFN	MLB	27	6	5	0	12	12	68¹	59	5	4.2	9.1	69	42%	.297
2017	SFN	MLB	28	6	15	0	32	31	174¹	200	27	3.5	7.6	148	39%	.320
2018	TEX	MLB	29	3	8	0	39	12	102	128	19	3.6	7.6	86	39%	.341
2019	DET	MLB	30	5	8	0	19	19	100²	110	16	3.4	7.3	82	39%	.301

Breakout: 35%   Improve: 55%   Collapse: 7%   Attrition: 10%   MLB: 84%
Comparables: Scott Kazmir, Luke Hochevar, Tim Leary

The professor did not look up from his book, but simply held one finger aloft until, one by one, his students noticed, and lowered their voices until the room was silent. Only then did the old man's eyes spark to life as he looked into the room of hopeful young students. "In 2011," he began, "a rookie pitcher from Tampa Bay torpedoed the mighty Texas Rangers in the first game of the ALDS, holding them to no runs and just two hits over seven innings en route to a 9-0 blowout."

A flutter of whispers skittered around the room like autumn leaves. Baseball? Where was he going with this?

"Seven years later, that very pitcher, no longer a rookie, of course, no longer a prospect, was traded to the Texas Rangers, and again torpedoed them, this time notching just one win before June, when he was relegated to the bullpen. Of what, dear students, is this an example?"

He lowered his glasses and peered at the collected students until he spotted one confident soul, hand aloft. "Yes?"

"It's irony, sir." the freshman said, assuredly.

"No, you fool," the professor snapped, then scoffed again for effect as he paced around his lectern.

"Tragedy?"

"Perhaps, if you believe in such things," the professor allowed, still pacing. "He was, by all accounts, a good man with a kind heart. But no, that's not the answer I'm looking for."

The room went silent, and the professor stopped pacing, looking for another volunteer, but the room had gone still.

"It's NIHILISM!" he shouted with an enthusiasm that felt more like spite than joy. "The Rays lost that series to the Rangers in 2011; the rookie's performance was for naught! And the 2018 Rangers were careening head-first into a rebuild, anyway. They took a shot at a reclamation project and it didn't pan out. None of it matters. On that note, you're all being given a failing grade. If you're a true student of philosophy, you'll be back tomorrow because you want to learn anyway. The rest of you who were only here for a grade would have dropped the class in a month anyway. You're all dismissed."

YEAR	TEAM	LVL	AGE	WHIP	ERA	DRA	WARP	MPH	FB%	WHF	CSP
2016	TBA	MLB	27	1.27	4.08	4.63	1.1	95.3	63	10.7	49.6
2016	SFN	MLB	27	1.33	4.08	3.86	1.2	95.4	63	12.3	48.5
2017	SFN	MLB	28	1.53	5.52	5.34	0.4	93.6	51.7	9.4	49.7
2018	TEX	MLB	29	1.66	6.79	7.00	-2.2	94.4	58.7	10.7	52.5
2019	DET	MLB	30	1.49	4.85	5.25	0.2	93.6	57.3	10.4	50.6

Matt Moore, continued

Pitch Shape vs LHH

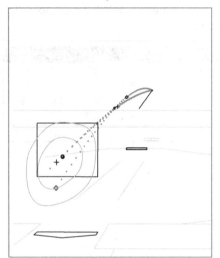

Pitch Shape vs RHH

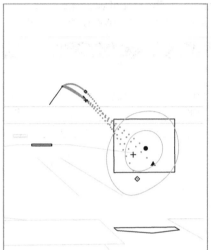

Type	Frequency	Velocity	H Movement	V Movement
● Fastball	58.3%	92.8 [101]	10.2 [84]	-15 [102]
□ Sinker	0.3%	92.2 [99]	11.8 [107]	-16 [114]
+ Cutter	9.2%	90.2 [109]	0.9 [84]	-19.2 [118]
▲ Changeup	13.4%	84 [95]	14.5 [83]	-28.4 [97]
✕ Splitter				
▽ Slider				
◇ Curveball	18.8%	81 [109]	-4.9 [88]	-47.6 [101]
⊕ Slow Curveball				
✳ Knuckleball				
▼ Screwball				

Daniel Norris LHP

Born: 04/25/93 Age: 26 Bats: L Throws: L
Height: 6'2" Weight: 185 Origin: Round 2, 2011 Draft (#74 overall)

YEAR	TEAM	LVL	AGE	W	L	SV	G	GS	IP	H	HR	BB/9	K/9	K	GB%	BABIP
2016	TOL	AAA	23	5	7	0	14	14	73¹	78	2	3.4	9.4	77	57%	.358
2016	DET	MLB	23	4	2	0	14	13	69¹	75	10	2.9	9.2	71	38%	.327
2017	TOL	AAA	24	0	4	0	6	6	14	22	3	10.3	11.6	18	50%	.442
2017	DET	MLB	24	5	8	0	22	18	101²	120	12	3.9	7.6	86	40%	.344
2018	DET	MLB	25	0	5	0	11	8	44¹	46	8	3.9	10.4	51	33%	.317
2019	*DET*	*MLB*	*26*	*5*	*7*	*0*	*19*	*19*	*95*	*95*	*12*	*3.7*	*9.0*	*95*	*41%*	*.305*

Breakout: 26% Improve: 57% Collapse: 15% Attrition: 13% MLB: 93%
Comparables: Luke Hochevar, Shaun Marcum, Jordan Zimmermann

2014: Elbow surgery.
2015: Strained oblique. (And in the offseason, thyroid cancer treatment.)
2016: Strained oblique.
2017: Strained oblique, vertebral hairline fractures, groin injury.
2018: Groin injury.
2019: Oh, let's say, the mumps.
2020: Ingrown belly button.
2021: Grows a dorsal fin, and then the dorsal fin hurts a lot.
2022: Becomes one of us, stays in a padded room, forever, playing *Bases Loaded* on the NES until the pain is gone.

YEAR	TEAM	LVL	AGE	WHIP	ERA	DRA	WARP	MPH	FB%	WHF	CSP
2016	TOL	AAA	23	1.45	4.54	3.45	1.6				
2016	DET	MLB	23	1.40	3.38	5.31	0.0	96.0	61.8	11.6	46
2017	TOL	AAA	24	2.71	12.21	4.62	0.2				
2017	DET	MLB	24	1.61	5.31	6.48	-1.1	94.8	55	10	45.1
2018	DET	MLB	25	1.47	5.68	5.12	0.1	92.1	52.7	11.4	49.4
2019	*DET*	*MLB*	*26*	*1.44*	*4.11*	*4.45*	*1.1*	*94.0*	*57*	*11*	*48*

Daniel Norris, continued

Pitch Shape vs LHH

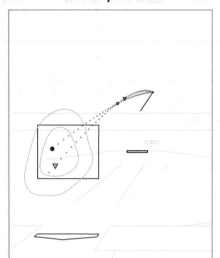

Pitch Shape vs RHH

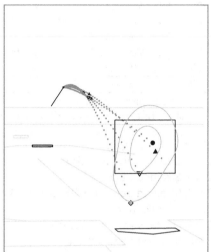

Type		Frequency	Velocity	H Movement	V Movement
●	Fastball	51.1%	90.7 [94]	4.3 [111]	-15.3 [102]
□	Sinker	1.6%	90.6 [91]	10.2 [120]	-17.1 [111]
+	Cutter				
▲	Changeup	5.9%	85 [99]	7.9 [118]	-31.1 [89]
✕	Splitter				
▽	Slider	35.7%	83.6 [96]	-4.8 [100]	-36.4 [90]
◇	Curveball	5.7%	76.6 [93]	-5.8 [91]	-57.2 [79]
⊕	Slow Curveball				
✳	Knuckleball				
▼	Screwball				

Tyson Ross RHP

Born: 04/22/87   Age: 32   Bats: R   Throws: R
Height: 6'6"   Weight: 245   Origin: Round 2, 2008 Draft (#58 overall)

YEAR	TEAM	LVL	AGE	W	L	SV	G	GS	IP	H	HR	BB/9	K/9	K	GB%	BABIP
2016	SDN	MLB	29	0	1	0	1	1	5¹	9	0	1.7	8.4	5	47%	.474
2017	ROU	AAA	30	2	1	0	4	4	18²	23	3	5.3	5.3	11	46%	.345
2017	FRI	AA	30	1	1	0	2	2	11²	11	0	3.1	7.7	10	62%	.324
2017	TEX	MLB	30	3	3	0	12	10	49	53	7	6.8	6.6	36	48%	.305
2018	SDN	MLB	31	6	9	0	22	22	123¹	112	16	3.8	7.8	107	45%	.276
2018	SLN	MLB	31	2	0	0	9	1	26¹	20	1	3.4	5.1	15	58%	.244
2019	DET	MLB	32	6	10	0	23	23	121	128	16	4.2	6.8	93	46%	.299

Breakout: 8%   Improve: 40%   Collapse: 23%   Attrition: 11%   MLB: 84%
Comparables: Doug Davis, Barry Zito, Carlos Zambrano

Ross proved he can still make it through a season (mostly) healthy. That's a moral victory for a pitcher who has survived both Tommy John surgery and thoracic outlet syndrome. More concrete victories, however, seem mostly beyond his reach now. His fastball now sits 91-92 mph, with less hop than a Yugoslavian center, and his slider isn't the whipsaw it used to be. Ross hasn't been an average big-league hurler — let alone the budding ace he was at his peak — since 2015, and there's nothing left in his arm to suggest that's going to change. Still, that's the life of a major-league pitcher: plush velvet sometimes, sometimes just pretzels and beer. So far, he's still here.

YEAR	TEAM	LVL	AGE	WHIP	ERA	DRA	WARP	MPH	FB%	WHF	CSP
2016	SDN	MLB	29	1.88	11.81	3.40	0.1	95.2	53.3	14.4	40.4
2017	ROU	AAA	30	1.82	7.71	5.26	0.1				
2017	FRI	AA	30	1.29	2.31	3.59	0.2				
2017	TEX	MLB	30	1.84	7.71	8.24	-1.5	93.7	57.1	7.7	41.1
2018	SDN	MLB	31	1.33	4.45	4.94	0.5	92.9	41.7	9.3	43.9
2018	SLN	MLB	31	1.14	2.73	5.50	-0.1	93.8	41.7	8.3	46.1
2019	DET	MLB	32	1.54	4.91	5.32	0.1	92.3	45	8.8	41.9

Tyson Ross, continued

Pitch Shape vs LHH

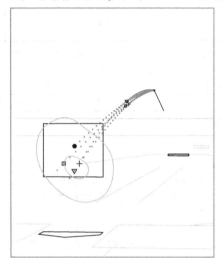

Pitch Shape vs RHH

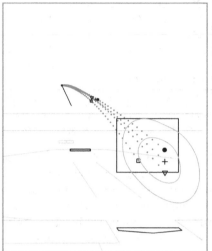

Type		Frequency	Velocity	H Movement	V Movement
●	Fastball	36.3%	91.7 [97]	-1.2 [125]	-17.7 [94]
□	Sinker	6.0%	91.6 [96]	-7.6 [141]	-22.4 [93]
+	Cutter	15.9%	89.9 [107]	0.9 [94]	-23.3 [102]
▲	Changeup	0.8%	86.8 [106]	-8.1 [117]	-26.6 [102]
✕	Splitter				
▽	Slider	40.9%	85.1 [103]	4.9 [100]	-33.6 [98]
◇	Curveball				
⊕	Slow Curveball				
✳	Knuckleball				
▼	Screwball				

Daniel Stumpf LHP

Born: 01/04/91   Age: 28   Bats: L   Throws: L
Height: 6'2"   Weight: 208   Origin: Round 9, 2012 Draft (#283 overall)

YEAR	TEAM	LVL	AGE	W	L	SV	G	GS	IP	H	HR	BB/9	K/9	K	GB%	BABIP
2016	PHI	MLB	25	0	0	0	7	0	5	9	1	3.6	3.6	2	38%	.400
2016	NWA	AA	25	2	0	1	14	0	21¹	14	0	1.7	11.0	26	55%	.264
2017	TOL	AAA	26	1	2	0	24	0	21¹	19	3	2.1	11.0	26	47%	.320
2017	DET	MLB	26	0	1	0	55	0	37²	37	5	3.6	7.9	33	43%	.305
2018	TOL	AAA	27	1	0	0	9	0	10¹	12	1	0.0	11.3	13	29%	.407
2018	DET	MLB	27	1	5	0	56	0	38¹	44	5	3.8	8.7	37	38%	.339
2019	*DET*	*MLB*	*28*	*2*	*2*	*0*	*43*	*0*	*45*	*46*	*7*	*3.7*	*8.3*	*42*	*43%*	*.303*

Breakout: 21%   Improve: 37%   Collapse: 18%   Attrition: 22%   MLB: 66%
Comparables: Mike Adams, Lucas Luetge, Jose Veras

Stumpf could be useful if he simply faced mostly lefties, offering a fastball-slider combination and keeping everything low in the zone. His numbers suffered in part due to being the lone southpaw for a rebuilding team with neither luxury nor device for a one-out guy, so he faced foes of both handedness equally. Because, you never know, he might turn out to be one of those weird "good" left-handers. Spoiler alert: he's not. He's a specialist, and now for the bad news: there are better ones out there.

YEAR	TEAM	LVL	AGE	WHIP	ERA	DRA	WARP	MPH	FB%	WHF	CSP
2016	PHI	MLB	25	2.20	10.80	3.66	0.1	95.1	38	14	47.5
2016	NWA	AA	25	0.84	2.11	2.46	0.6				
2017	TOL	AAA	26	1.12	3.38	2.66	0.6				
2017	DET	MLB	26	1.38	3.82	5.78	-0.3	95.2	60.2	8.2	48.3
2018	TOL	AAA	27	1.16	3.48	3.60	0.2				
2018	DET	MLB	27	1.57	4.93	3.44	0.7	95.4	53.7	12.4	46.2
2019	*DET*	*MLB*	*28*	*1.45*	*4.88*	*5.00*	*0.1*	*94.7*	*55.9*	*10.8*	*47.5*

Daniel Stumpf, continued

Pitch Shape vs LHH

Pitch Shape vs RHH

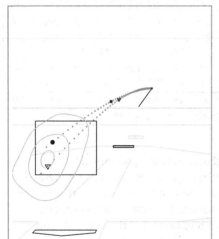
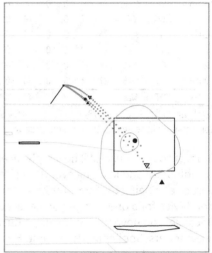

Type	Frequency	Velocity	H Movement	V Movement
● Fastball	53.7%	93.8 [104]	9.5 [87]	-14.3 [105]
□ Sinker				
+ Cutter				
▲ Changeup	4.7%	86.5 [105]	14.1 [85]	-27.6 [99]
✕ Splitter				
▽ Slider	41.6%	85.2 [104]	-0.9 [83]	-29.8 [110]
◇ Curveball				
⊕ Slow Curveball				
✳ Knuckleball				
▼ Screwball				

Spencer Turnbull   RHP

Born: 09/18/92   Age: 26   Bats: R   Throws: R
Height: 6'3"   Weight: 215   Origin: Round 2, 2014 Draft (#63 overall)

YEAR	TEAM	LVL	AGE	W	L	SV	G	GS	IP	H	HR	BB/9	K/9	K	GB%	BABIP
2016	TGW	RK	23	0	1	0	4	4	10²	3	0	4.2	5.9	7	69%	.115
2016	LAK	A+	23	1	1	0	6	6	30	24	1	3.0	8.1	27	56%	.274
2017	LAK	A+	24	7	3	0	15	15	82²	68	3	2.7	7.0	64	52%	.280
2017	ERI	AA	24	0	3	0	4	4	20¹	22	1	3.5	9.7	22	58%	.356
2018	ERI	AA	25	4	7	0	19	19	98²	92	4	3.6	9.6	105	56%	.332
2018	TOL	AAA	25	1	1	0	2	2	13¹	8	0	2.0	12.8	19	57%	.267
2018	DET	MLB	25	0	2	0	4	3	16¹	17	1	2.2	8.3	15	48%	.327
2019	DET	MLB	26	2	3	0	27	6	52²	50	6	4.0	8.6	50	50%	.297

Breakout: 11%   Improve: 29%   Collapse: 16%   Attrition: 36%   MLB: 54%
Comparables: Sean Nolin, Samuel Gaviglio, Jack Egbert

Prospects don't linearly traipse through an organization, as much as we'd like to pretend. Sometimes there's a setback, be it injury or self-inflicted struggle. Other times someone is rushed ahead to the finish line. Turnbull felt both sides of that progression, overcoming a midseason injury to scoot out of Double-A and into the majors by September. For funsies, he started the final game of the season against the playoff-bound Brewers, who needed the win to force an NL Central tiebreaker. They predictably broke him, but Turnbull will again rebound with a strong chance to start in 2019, featuring a power sinker and plenty of peripheral pitches that have caused off-balance swings throughout his career.

YEAR	TEAM	LVL	AGE	WHIP	ERA	DRA	WARP	MPH	FB%	WHF	CSP
2016	TGW	RK	23	0.75	3.38	4.54	0.1				
2016	LAK	A+	23	1.13	3.00	3.22	0.8				
2017	LAK	A+	24	1.12	3.05	3.20	2.0				
2017	ERI	AA	24	1.48	6.20	4.48	0.2				
2018	ERI	AA	25	1.34	4.47	3.73	1.8				
2018	TOL	AAA	25	0.82	2.03	2.57	0.4				
2018	DET	MLB	25	1.29	6.06	4.99	0.1	96.1	66.7	9.9	49.3
2019	DET	MLB	26	1.39	4.10	4.42	0.5	95.7	67.9	10.1	50.2

Spencer Turnbull, continued

Pitch Shape vs LHH

Pitch Shape vs RHH

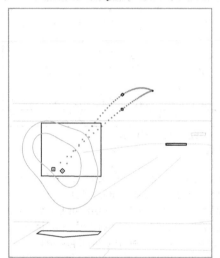
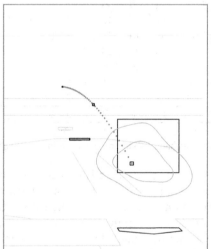

Type		Frequency	Velocity	H Movement	V Movement
●	Fastball	11.0%	94.1 [105]	-1.2 [125]	-18.3 [92]
□	Sinker	43.6%	94.8 [111]	-13.9 [89]	-21.5 [96]
+	Cutter	12.1%	93 [125]	-0.5 [86]	-20.3 [114]
▲	Changeup	5.0%	88 [111]	-15.5 [77]	-28.7 [96]
✕	Splitter				
▽	Slider	10.3%	89.1 [121]	3.7 [95]	-26.3 [120]
◇	Curveball	18.1%	81.5 [111]	7.3 [98]	-46.5 [104]
⊕	Slow Curveball				
✳	Knuckleball				
▼	Screwball				

Drew VerHagen RHP

Born: 10/22/90   Age: 28   Bats: R   Throws: R
Height: 6'6"   Weight: 230   Origin: Round 4, 2012 Draft (#154 overall)

YEAR	TEAM	LVL	AGE	W	L	SV	G	GS	IP	H	HR	BB/9	K/9	K	GB%	BABIP
2016	DET	MLB	25	1	0	0	19	0	19	28	3	3.3	4.7	10	60%	.362
2017	TOL	AAA	26	7	7	0	19	19	97¹	108	7	4.0	6.4	69	46%	.329
2017	DET	MLB	26	0	3	0	24	2	34¹	42	10	2.4	6.6	25	51%	.317
2018	TOL	AAA	27	2	1	0	10	6	32²	18	0	2.8	14.1	51	52%	.273
2018	DET	MLB	27	3	3	0	41	1	56¹	46	6	3.0	8.5	53	48%	.263
2019	DET	MLB	28	2	3	0	54	0	56	50	5	3.6	8.8	56	48%	.291

Breakout: 21%   Improve: 41%   Collapse: 10%   Attrition: 21%   MLB: 70%
Comparables: Troy Patton, Darrell Rasner, Nathan Adcock

The idea of VerHagen as a starter may never completely abandon him, as he can work multiple innings and keep the ball on the ground. That much we know. Yes, the big man works off his sinker, and his iffy additional pitches kept him away from the rotation, but the catch-22 is he was the Tigers' most useful middle reliever *because* of those other offerings, namely the slider and curve. Need more evidence? He was given one start last year, allowing three home runs — equal to his total in 52 2/3 reliever innings. Yeah, keep him in the bullpen.

YEAR	TEAM	LVL	AGE	WHIP	ERA	DRA	WARP	MPH	FB%	WHF	CSP
2016	DET	MLB	25	1.84	7.11	5.55	-0.1	97.0	62.7	7.6	46.6
2017	TOL	AAA	26	1.55	4.90	4.67	1.1				
2017	DET	MLB	26	1.49	5.77	4.95	0.1	95.5	60.5	9.6	50.2
2018	TOL	AAA	27	0.86	1.65	2.89	1.0				
2018	DET	MLB	27	1.15	4.63	3.79	0.8	95.8	54	12.7	46.8
2019	DET	MLB	28	1.28	3.68	4.05	0.7	95.3	57.3	11.2	48.1

Drew VerHagen, continued

Pitch Shape vs LHH

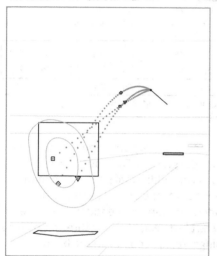

Pitch Shape vs RHH

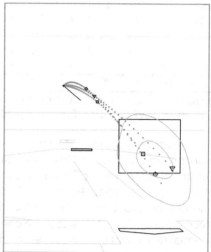

Type		Frequency	Velocity	H Movement	V Movement
●	Fastball	4.7%	94.9 [108]	-0.7 [128]	-14.1 [105]
□	Sinker	49.3%	94.6 [110]	-11.3 [111]	-18.3 [107]
+	Cutter				
▲	Changeup	0.7%	90.2 [120]	-8.4 [115]	-20.3 [121]
×	Splitter				
▽	Slider	28.8%	86.3 [108]	7.1 [110]	-33.7 [98]
◇	Curveball	16.6%	80 [106]	9.3 [106]	-52.7 [90]
⊕	Slow Curveball				
✳	Knuckleball				
▼	Screwball				

Jordan Zimmermann RHP

Born: 05/23/86   Age: 33   Bats: R   Throws: R
Height: 6'2"   Weight: 225   Origin: Round 2, 2007 Draft (#67 overall)

YEAR	TEAM	LVL	AGE	W	L	SV	G	GS	IP	H	HR	BB/9	K/9	K	GB%	BABIP
2016	TOL	AAA	30	0	1	0	5	5	20¹	19	2	1.8	4.9	11	46%	.270
2016	DET	MLB	30	9	7	0	19	18	105¹	118	14	2.2	5.6	66	44%	.304
2017	DET	MLB	31	8	13	0	29	29	160	204	29	2.5	5.8	103	35%	.330
2018	DET	MLB	32	7	8	0	25	25	131¹	140	28	1.8	7.6	111	37%	.288
2019	*DET*	*MLB*	*33*	*7*	*12*	*0*	*28*	*28*	*159*	*179*	*28*	*2.5*	*6.5*	*116*	*39%*	*.301*

Breakout: 24%   Improve: 47%   Collapse: 18%   Attrition: 10%   MLB: 86%
Comparables: Kyle Lohse, Aaron Harang, Rodrigo Lopez

He improved strongly last year, because it would have been difficult to sustain that awful 2017, though at this point Zimmermann and his contract are sunk costs. His fastball is in steady decline and is a favorite delicacy among those carrying baseball bats in the American League Central. It's rated highly on Yelp ("A must try! Goes high and far!") and there are plenty of portions to go around. His slider is workable, and on days it snaps like Michael rebooting *The Good Place* he'll go deep into the game and scribes will pine about his potential comeback. His strikeout and walk rates have stabilized, which means he can still operate as a fourth starter. He just needs to take the fastball off the menu or just garnish it with something.

YEAR	TEAM	LVL	AGE	WHIP	ERA	DRA	WARP	MPH	FB%	WHF	CSP
2016	TOL	AAA	30	1.13	1.33	3.53	0.4				
2016	DET	MLB	30	1.37	4.87	4.52	1.0	94.3	52.8	8.5	49.2
2017	DET	MLB	31	1.55	6.07	6.90	-2.4	93.5	54.2	8.8	51.3
2018	DET	MLB	32	1.26	4.52	4.76	0.8	92.5	45.3	9.9	48.2
2019	*DET*	*MLB*	*33*	*1.41*	*4.86*	*5.26*	*0.3*	*92.2*	*49.8*	*9.1*	*48.9*

Jordan Zimmermann, continued

Pitch Shape vs LHH

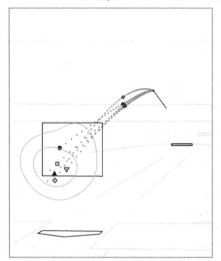

Pitch Shape vs RHH

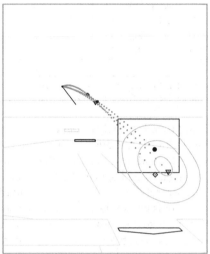

Type		Frequency	Velocity	H Movement	V Movement
●	Fastball	43.1%	91.7 [97]	-5.9 [103]	-15.1 [102]
□	Sinker	2.2%	91.5 [95]	-12.3 [102]	-21.7 [96]
+	Cutter				
▲	Changeup	5.5%	87.1 [107]	-12 [96]	-26.8 [102]
✕	Splitter				
▽	Slider	33.2%	87.2 [112]	3.3 [93]	-25.1 [124]
◇	Curveball	16.0%	80.9 [109]	5.2 [89]	-42.5 [113]
⊕	Slow Curveball				
✳	Knuckleball				
▼	Screwball				

Daz Cameron CF

Born: 01/15/97 Age: 22 Bats: R Throws: R
Height: 6'2" Weight: 195 Origin: Round 1, 2015 Draft (#37 overall)

YEAR	TEAM	LVL	AGE	PA	R	2B	3B	HR	RBI	BB	K	SB	CS	AVG/OBP/SLG
2016	QUD	A	19	87	5	2	2	0	6	8	33	4	3	.143/.221/.221
2016	TCV	A-	19	89	13	3	1	2	14	6	26	8	2	.278/.352/.418
2017	QUD	A	20	511	79	29	8	14	73	45	108	32	12	.271/.349/.466
2018	LAK	A+	21	246	35	9	3	3	20	25	69	10	4	.259/.346/.370
2018	ERI	AA	21	226	32	12	5	5	35	25	53	12	5	.285/.367/.470
2018	TOL	AAA	21	62	8	4	1	0	6	2	15	2	2	.211/.246/.316
2019	DET	MLB	22	251	29	8	2	6	21	14	77	7	3	.185/.236/.315

Breakout: 4% Improve: 14% Collapse: 0% Attrition: 10% MLB: 20%
Comparables: Kirk Nieuwenhuis, Ryan Kalish, Michael Saunders

Depending on how well he does in Triple-A this year, Cameron might force his way onto a major-league roster in September, reaching the bigs at the same age as Pops did for the White Sox in 1995. He moved quickly last year, thanks to playing an exceptional center field along with some plus speed. The bat-to-ball skills have always been the question mark for the former first-round pick acquired from the Astros in the Justin Verlander trade, but he checked that box as a 21-year-old in Double-A. While his tool mix likely won't put Cameron at the top of the lineup, his opportunity at the highest level should arrive sooner rather than later.

YEAR	TEAM	LVL	AGE	PA	DRC+	VORP	BABIP	BRR	FRAA	WARP
2016	QUD	A	19	87	40	-5.6	.244	0.1	CF(10): -0.6, LF(6): -0.3	-0.6
2016	TCV	A-	19	89	111	4.7	.392	0.0	CF(15): 0.0, LF(2): -0.3	0.1
2017	QUD	A	20	511	132	38.4	.323	3.1	CF(110): 1.8, RF(4): 0.1	3.2
2018	LAK	A+	21	246	117	9.9	.366	2.5	CF(38): 1.9, RF(18): 0.9	1.2
2018	ERI	AA	21	226	124	11.4	.366	3.4	CF(34): -7.0, RF(16): 1.5	0.7
2018	TOL	AAA	21	62	55	-1.1	.279	0.7	CF(14): 0.3, RF(1): 0.0	-0.1
2019	DET	MLB	22	251	47	-6.5	.243	0.6	CF -1, RF 0	-0.7

Derek Hill CF

Born: 12/30/95   Age: 23   Bats: R   Throws: R
Height: 6'2"   Weight: 190   Origin: Round 1, 2014 Draft (#23 overall)

YEAR	TEAM	LVL	AGE	PA	R	2B	3B	HR	RBI	BB	K	SB	CS	AVG/OBP/SLG
2016	WMI	A	20	415	66	17	6	1	31	24	105	35	6	.266/.312/.349
2017	TGW	RK	21	61	11	1	1	1	7	10	15	7	0	.163/.300/.286
2017	WMI	A	21	168	28	8	6	1	21	16	38	12	5	.285/.367/.444
2017	LAK	A+	21	38	3	1	0	0	2	5	10	10	0	.194/.324/.226
2018	LAK	A+	22	383	45	9	3	4	33	33	109	35	12	.239/.307/.318
2019	DET	MLB	23	251	29	5	1	5	17	10	81	12	3	.182/.217/.277

Breakout: 4%   Improve: 5%   Collapse: 0%   Attrition: 5%   MLB: 5%
Comparables: Adam Engel, Michael Taylor, Lane Adams

So far it's been rough seas for Hill, a former first-round pick who's yet to reach Double-A and remains overmatched at the plate. If he can sneak one of those novelty wiffle ball bats to the plate — and it's unlikely he will, as umpires usually notice such gambits — he may fix that batting average. He did, however, lead the Florida State League in stolen bases, which has always been his meal ticket. His defense is also major league-ready and may have been ready when he was a teenager, which is why the team is going to stay patient.

YEAR	TEAM	LVL	AGE	PA	DRC+	VORP	BABIP	BRR	FRAA	WARP
2016	WMI	A	20	415	96	16.6	.361	6.6	CF(54): -6.7, RF(33): 5.1	0.8
2017	TGW	RK	21	61	69	2.2	.206	1.2	CF(7): 0.6	0.0
2017	WMI	A	21	168	115	15.0	.374	2.2	CF(23): 0.1	0.7
2017	LAK	A+	21	38	86	3.0	.286	1.5	CF(6): -0.1	0.1
2018	LAK	A+	22	383	82	5.4	.338	3.7	CF(55): -2.5, LF(27): -2.1	-0.5
2019	DET	MLB	23	251	28	-11.5	.247	1.8	CF -1, LF 0	-1.3

Parker Meadows CF

Born: 11/02/99   Age: 19   Bats: L   Throws: R
Height: 6'5"   Weight: 185   Origin: Round 2, 2018 Draft (#44 overall)

YEAR	TEAM	LVL	AGE	PA	R	2B	3B	HR	RBI	BB	K	SB	CS	AVG/OBP/SLG
2018	TGW	RK	18	85	16	2	1	4	8	8	25	3	1	.284/.376/.500
2019	DET	MLB	19	251	18	3	0	8	25	4	103	1	0	.144/.157/.253

Breakout: 5%   Improve: 7%   Collapse: 0%   Attrition: 3%   MLB: 9%
Comparables: Engel Beltre, Nomar Mazara, Carlos Tocci

Detroit drafted Meadows, who slipped to the second round due to his commitment to play college ball at Clemson. However, after being offered $2.5 million to skip class, he chose the Tigers instead of the Tigers. He wasn't drafted as high as his brother Austin (2013 first round, now with the Rays), but he did copy big bro in being a left-handed-hitting center fielder with some potentially next-level power and speed. Brotherly rivalries are always fun to watch blossom, so while Parker is behind his major-league big brother in several categories (except height), we have seen his story play out before: in six years they'll both wind up in the Braves outfield and it's going to go horribly wrong.

YEAR	TEAM	LVL	AGE	PA	DRC+	VORP	BABIP	BRR	FRAA	WARP
2018	TGW	RK	18	85	126	6.1	.378	0.0	CF(20): -3.1	-0.1
2019	DET	MLB	19	251	1	-20.7	.201	-0.4	CF -1	-2.3

Isaac Paredes 3B

Born: 02/18/99   Age: 20   Bats: R   Throws: R
Height: 5'11"   Weight: 225   Origin: International Free Agent, 2015

YEAR	TEAM	LVL	AGE	PA	R	2B	3B	HR	RBI	BB	K	SB	CS	AVG/OBP/SLG
2016	CUB	RK	17	185	23	14	3	1	26	13	20	4	0	.305/.359/.443
2017	SBN	A	18	384	49	25	0	7	49	29	54	2	1	.264/.343/.401
2017	WMI	A	18	133	16	3	0	4	21	13	13	0	0	.217/.323/.348
2018	LAK	A+	19	347	50	19	2	12	48	32	54	1	0	.259/.338/.455
2018	ERI	AA	19	155	20	9	0	3	22	19	22	1	0	.321/.406/.458
2019	DET	MLB	20	251	21	10	0	7	26	11	53	0	0	.187/.235/.317

Breakout: 17%   Improve: 27%   Collapse: 0%   Attrition: 6%   MLB: 27%
Comparables: Jurickson Profar, Carlos Correa, J.P. Crawford

Paredes was the "other" prospect, along with Jeimer Candelario, acquired in the deal that sent Alex Avila and Justin Wilson to the Cubs. He reached Double-A as a 19-year-old and thrived there for the final month-and-a-half of the season, showing the type of advanced hitting ability that may ultimately turn Candelario into the "other" prospect. He's unlikely to stick at shortstop given his stocky build and modest range, but should have more than enough arm for third base. Offensively he projects to have good, solid skills across the board, with plenty of time left to show that he has more upside than that.

YEAR	TEAM	LVL	AGE	PA	DRC+	VORP	BABIP	BRR	FRAA	WARP
2016	CUB	RK	17	185	149	15.6	.338	-0.3	SS(45): 6.6	1.5
2017	SBN	A	18	384	111	17.4	.294	-1.0	SS(70): -2.7, 3B(7): 2.5	1.2
2017	WMI	A	18	133	110	0.2	.214	-0.5	SS(22): -2.4, 3B(5): 1.4	0.4
2018	LAK	A+	19	347	127	24.2	.274	0.3	SS(59): 3.2, 2B(22): 0.5	2.0
2018	ERI	AA	19	155	141	13.7	.358	0.3	3B(18): 0.6, SS(15): 0.9	1.2
2019	DET	MLB	20	251	47	-7.7	.211	-0.5	SS 0, 2B 0	-0.7

Wenceel Perez   SS

Born: 10/30/99   Age: 19   Bats: B   Throws: R
Height: 5'11"   Weight: 170   Origin: International Free Agent, 2016

YEAR	TEAM	LVL	AGE	PA	R	2B	3B	HR	RBI	BB	K	SB	CS	AVG/OBP/SLG
2017	DTI	RK	17	258	31	8	1	0	22	27	21	16	6	.314/.387/.358
2018	TGW	RK	18	93	20	7	0	2	14	12	14	2	1	.383/.462/.543
2018	ONE	A-	18	87	8	2	0	1	8	5	12	7	3	.244/.287/.305
2018	WMI	A	18	71	8	3	3	0	9	2	8	4	1	.309/.324/.441
2019	DET	MLB	19	251	24	4	1	5	18	7	57	5	2	.175/.195/.258

Breakout: 4%   Improve: 5%   Collapse: 0%   Attrition: 3%   MLB: 6%
Comparables: Carlos Triunfel, Wilmer Flores, Gleyber Torres

The Gulf Coast League was getting sick of Perez, the 18-year-old switch-hitting shortstop who signed into the Tigers organization in 2016 thanks to a cool half-mil bonus. He was hitting the ball everywhere, except beyond the fence and toward the fielders, and was rewarded with a push into full-season ball, where he still peppered the outfield. He should progress and maintain a high level of middle-infield defense and an exemplary bat-to-ball skill. And you've been very patient, so your reward for reading to the end: his first name rhymes with "pencil."

YEAR	TEAM	LVL	AGE	PA	DRC+	VORP	BABIP	BRR	FRAA	WARP
2017	DTI	RK	17	258	118	16.0	.343	2.6	SS(50): -6.8, 2B(11): 2.4	1.0
2018	TGW	RK	18	93	211	14.4	.446	0.6	SS(19): 1.0	1.2
2018	ONE	A-	18	87	124	2.0	.275	0.3	SS(21): -2.9	0.0
2018	WMI	A	18	71	104	4.8	.344	0.1	SS(14): -0.6	0.2
2019	DET	MLB	19	251	20	-14.2	.205	0.4	SS -3	-1.8

Dustin Peterson   OF

Born: 09/10/94   Age: 24   Bats: R   Throws: R
Height: 6'2"   Weight: 210   Origin: Round 2, 2013 Draft (#50 overall)

YEAR	TEAM	LVL	AGE	PA	R	2B	3B	HR	RBI	BB	K	SB	CS	AVG/OBP/SLG
2016	MIS	AA	21	578	65	38	2	12	88	45	100	4	1	.282/.343/.431
2017	GWN	AAA	22	346	35	17	1	1	30	27	78	1	2	.248/.318/.318
2018	ATL	MLB	23	2	0	0	0	0	0	0	1	0	0	.000/.000/.000
2018	GWN	AAA	23	442	46	23	0	11	55	30	96	3	0	.268/.324/.406
2019	DET	MLB	24	102	9	5	0	2	10	5	25	0	0	.221/.265/.337

Breakout: 10%   Improve: 19%   Collapse: 1%   Attrition: 24%   MLB: 34%
Comparables: Bryan Petersen, Jake Cave, Shane Peterson

It's been five years since Peterson was one of four players acquired for Justin Upton. It's also four years since a bus crash with the Carolina Mudcats put him on the disabled list and two years since hand surgery for a non-bus-related injury. In between doctor visits, he has neither blown away nor disappointed his superiors, which means he's steadily moved up the minor-league gauntlet and received exactly two major-league pinch-hit appearances. He also snagged the Gwinnett Stripers' "Most Competitive Player" award, which is a real thing, before being let go in a September waiver claim. He has just enough youth, power, speed, scars and bat-to-ball skills to warrant being a fifth outfielder.

YEAR	TEAM	LVL	AGE	PA	DRC+	VORP	BABIP	BRR	FRAA	WARP
2016	MIS	AA	21	578	123	37.1	.327	0.1	LF(125): -1.1, CF(4): -1.2	1.4
2017	GWN	AAA	22	346	78	-4.1	.328	0.1	LF(68): 6.4, RF(9): -0.4	0.1
2018	ATL	MLB	23	2	91	-0.5	.000	0.0		0.0
2018	GWN	AAA	23	442	105	11.1	.327	1.6	LF(65): -2.2, RF(34): 1.0	0.6
2019	DET	MLB	24	102	58	-2.8	.272	-0.2	LF 0, RF 0	-0.2

Jake Rogers C

Born: 04/18/95   Age: 24   Bats: R   Throws: R
Height: 6'1"   Weight: 190   Origin: Round 3, 2016 Draft (#97 overall)

YEAR	TEAM	LVL	AGE	PA	R	2B	3B	HR	RBI	BB	K	SB	CS	AVG/OBP/SLG
2016	TCV	A-	21	104	11	7	1	2	12	13	18	0	2	.253/.369/.425
2016	QUD	A	21	82	7	3	1	1	4	8	25	1	0	.208/.305/.319
2017	QUD	A	22	116	17	7	1	6	15	9	28	1	0	.255/.336/.520
2017	BCA	A+	22	367	43	18	3	12	55	44	72	13	8	.265/.357/.457
2018	ERI	AA	23	408	57	15	1	17	56	41	112	7	1	.219/.305/.412
2019	DET	MLB	24	67	6	2	0	2	7	5	20	1	0	.164/.235/.295

Breakout: 6%   Improve: 11%   Collapse: 0%   Attrition: 12%   MLB: 18%
Comparables: Andrew Knapp, Michael McKenry, Josh Donaldson

Rogers is not here to make friends, which is why he was essentially the Eastern League's hall monitor, throwing out 50 baserunners on 90 steal attempts, 20 more than anyone

YEAR	TEAM	P. COUNT	FRM RUNS	BLK RUNS	THRW RUNS	TOT RUNS
2018	ERI	13801	20.3	-0.4	7.2	28.0
2019	DET	2451	1.8	-0.3	0.6	2.1

else in the EL. (As a comparison, no *major*-league catcher has thrown out 50 baserunners in a season in 15 years.) His golden arm is accompanied by another arm, which when used in tandem is able to perform another fun baseball feat: home runs. His otherwise complete inability to make contact in any other fashion with regularity will keep him from becoming Buster Posey, but the defense will certainly be his hall pass to the majors.

YEAR	TEAM	LVL	AGE	PA	DRC+	VORP	BABIP	BRR	FRAA	WARP
2016	TCV	A-	21	104	127	4.3	.299	-2.0	C(24): 0.1	0.3
2016	QUD	A	21	82	81	1.6	.304	-0.7	C(19): -0.1	0.0
2017	QUD	A	22	116	129	10.2	.290	0.3	C(21): 0.9	0.8
2017	BCA	A+	22	367	133	30.2	.302	-0.8	C(63): 1.4	2.0
2018	ERI	AA	23	408	88	20.8	.261	2.7	C(98): 29.4, 1B(1): 0.0	4.2
2019	DET	MLB	24	67	40	-1.7	.212	0.0	C 2	0.0

Beau Burrows RHP

Born: 09/18/96   Age: 22   Bats: R   Throws: R
Height: 6'2"   Weight: 200   Origin: Round 1, 2015 Draft (#22 overall)

YEAR	TEAM	LVL	AGE	W	L	SV	G	GS	IP	H	HR	BB/9	K/9	K	GB%	BABIP
2016	WMI	A	19	6	4	0	21	20	97	87	2	2.8	6.2	67	42%	.283
2017	LAK	A+	20	4	3	0	11	11	58²	45	3	1.7	9.5	62	45%	.298
2017	ERI	AA	20	6	4	0	15	15	76¹	79	5	3.9	8.8	75	40%	.339
2018	ERI	AA	21	10	9	0	26	26	134	126	12	3.8	8.5	127	32%	.310
2019	DET	MLB	22	6	9	0	23	23	111	113	18	3.7	8.1	100	35%	.298

Breakout: 5%   Improve: 9%   Collapse: 7%   Attrition: 10%   MLB: 20%
Comparables: Reynaldo Lopez, Joe Ross, Chris Flexen

Burrows' lively fastball will propel him to the major leagues soon, and it's going to make him a starter. His Double-A numbers, while unspectacular, weren't too alarming, though his name does take us all the way back to the 1930s. The curveball plays well, and with changeups and sliders simmerin' in his crockpot, his secondary offerings will likely sustain success in the rotation. He plays often in the air, and has yet to get burned by the long ball (though it's the Eastern League, nobody does), but his floor potential is pretty lofty, about as lofty as having the name Beau in 2019.

YEAR	TEAM	LVL	AGE	WHIP	ERA	DRA	WARP	MPH	FB%	WHF	CSP
2016	WMI	A	19	1.21	3.15	3.87	1.3				
2017	LAK	A+	20	0.95	1.23	3.14	1.5				
2017	ERI	AA	20	1.47	4.72	4.38	0.7				
2018	ERI	AA	21	1.36	4.10	6.93	-2.5				
2019	DET	MLB	22	1.44	5.09	5.32	0.2				

Alex Faedo   RHP

Born: 11/12/95   Age: 23   Bats: R   Throws: R
Height: 6'5"   Weight: 230   Origin: Round 1, 2017 Draft (#18 overall)

YEAR	TEAM	LVL	AGE	W	L	SV	G	GS	IP	H	HR	BB/9	K/9	K	GB%	BABIP
2018	LAK	A+	22	2	4	0	12	12	61	49	3	1.9	7.5	51	33%	.263
2018	ERI	AA	22	3	6	0	12	12	60	54	15	3.3	8.9	59	28%	.250
2019	DET	MLB	23	4	7	0	16	16	81	84	16	3.2	7.5	67	30%	.285

Breakout: 2%   Improve: 6%   Collapse: 16%   Attrition: 19%   MLB: 28%
Comparables: Wes Parsons, Jon Gray, Brett Kennedy

Slight worry simmered throughout the coterie of prospect wonks when Faedo's velocity went from high to low 90s. The organizational brass was not so much concerned, because baseball is literally outdoors poker, though his numbers definitely went south as he moved north. Sometimes the simplest explanation is the most obvious one: Faedo recorded a video of him tasting one of the Erie Seawolves' featured concession stand items, a hot dog wrapped in cotton candy and Nerds. Well, yea, that'll cause anyone's fastball to shrivel up. He'll probably try Double-A again, though the 2017 first-round pick's ceiling remains as a very strong starting pitcher with multiple offerings.

YEAR	TEAM	LVL	AGE	WHIP	ERA	DRA	WARP	MPH	FB%	WHF	CSP
2018	LAK	A+	22	1.02	3.10	3.19	1.5				
2018	ERI	AA	22	1.27	4.95	4.38	0.7				
2019	DET	MLB	23	1.39	5.47	5.73	-0.2				

Kyle Funkhouser RHP

Born: 03/16/94   Age: 25   Bats: R   Throws: R
Height: 6'2"   Weight: 220   Origin: Round 4, 2016 Draft (#115 overall)

YEAR	TEAM	LVL	AGE	W	L	SV	G	GS	IP	H	HR	BB/9	K/9	K	GB%	BABIP
2016	ONE	A-	22	0	2	0	13	13	37¹	34	0	1.9	8.2	34	53%	.324
2017	WMI	A	23	4	1	0	7	7	31¹	30	3	3.7	14.1	49	56%	.403
2017	LAK	A+	23	1	1	0	5	5	31¹	23	1	1.7	9.8	34	57%	.275
2018	ERI	AA	24	4	5	0	17	17	89	88	10	3.9	9.0	89	44%	.326
2018	TOL	AAA	24	0	2	0	2	2	8²	8	0	10.4	7.3	7	54%	.333
2019	DET	MLB	25	4	6	0	17	17	77	78	11	3.7	8.2	71	44%	.305

Breakout: 11%   Improve: 19%   Collapse: 12%   Attrition: 30%   MLB: 38%
Comparables: Matt Maloney, George Kontos, Jeff Niemann

The burly righty spent the year honing his secondary stuff to augment his upper-90s heat, earning a Double-A All-Star nod and a Triple-A promotion. Funkhouser's season ended abruptly when he fractured his foot on an uneven sidewalk walking home from Toledo's ballpark. Usually when coaches tell a minor-league pitcher to cut down on their walks, they don't mean it literally. It was the second physical setback in as many seasons for the former fourth-round pick, but his profile as a starter with three solid pitches remains unfunked.

YEAR	TEAM	LVL	AGE	WHIP	ERA	DRA	WARP	MPH	FB%	WHF	CSP
2016	ONE	A-	22	1.12	2.65	3.04	1.0				
2017	WMI	A	23	1.37	3.16	3.18	0.8				
2017	LAK	A+	23	0.93	1.72	2.97	0.8				
2018	ERI	AA	24	1.43	3.74	4.01	1.4				
2018	TOL	AAA	24	2.08	6.23	3.71	0.2				
2019	DET	MLB	25	1.43	4.71	4.91	0.5				

Matt Manning   RHP

Born: 01/28/98   Age: 21   Bats: R   Throws: R
Height: 6'6"   Weight: 190   Origin: Round 1, 2016 Draft (#9 overall)

YEAR	TEAM	LVL	AGE	W	L	SV	G	GS	IP	H	HR	BB/9	K/9	K	GB%	BABIP
2016	TGW	RK	18	0	2	0	10	10	29¹	27	2	2.1	14.1	46	38%	.379
2017	ONE	A-	19	2	2	0	9	9	33¹	27	0	3.8	9.7	36	31%	.310
2017	WMI	A	19	2	0	0	5	5	17²	14	0	5.6	13.2	26	49%	.341
2018	WMI	A	20	3	3	0	11	11	55²	47	3	4.5	12.3	76	43%	.344
2018	LAK	A+	20	4	4	0	9	9	51¹	32	4	3.3	11.4	65	47%	.241
2018	ERI	AA	20	0	1	0	2	2	10²	11	0	3.4	11.0	13	46%	.393
2019	DET	MLB	21	5	7	0	20	20	86	80	11	4.4	9.5	91	38%	.301

Breakout: 5%   Improve: 9%   Collapse: 2%   Attrition: 7%   MLB: 15%
Comparables: Sean Reid-Foley, Michael Kopech, Mike Montgomery

The most polarizing Tigers prospect since Steven Moya, Manning will be given every chance to remain a starting pitcher. In only three of his 22 starts last year did he fail to record fewer than one strikeout per inning (and all three were barely below the threshold), because the fastball is a weapon and the curveball is becoming more consistent. He's going to be a major-league pitcher at some point, and especially these days there's no shame in carving out a niche as a reliever. However, the Tigers are going to force the former no. 9 overall pick to fail into the 'pen.

YEAR	TEAM	LVL	AGE	WHIP	ERA	DRA	WARP	MPH	FB%	WHF	CSP
2016	TGW	RK	18	1.16	3.99	2.54	1.0				
2017	ONE	A-	19	1.23	1.89	3.75	0.6				
2017	WMI	A	19	1.42	5.60	3.43	0.4				
2018	WMI	A	20	1.35	3.40	3.23	1.3				
2018	LAK	A+	20	0.99	2.98	3.69	1.0				
2018	ERI	AA	20	1.41	4.22	3.06	0.3				
2019	DET	MLB	21	1.43	4.56	4.75	0.7				

Casey Mize   RHP

Born: 05/01/97   Age: 22   Bats: R   Throws: R
Height: 6'3"   Weight: 220   Origin: Round 1, 2018 Draft (#1 overall)

YEAR	TEAM	LVL	AGE	W	L	SV	G	GS	IP	H	HR	BB/9	K/9	K	GB%	BABIP
2018	LAK	A+	21	0	1	0	4	4	11²	13	2	1.5	7.7	10	44%	.344
2019	DET	MLB	22	2	3	0	8	8	33²	35	5	3.6	7.5	28	42%	.301

Breakout: 2%   Improve: 3%   Collapse: 0%   Attrition: 2%   MLB: 3%
Comparables: Jace Fry, Michael Ynoa, Chi Chi Gonzalez

Mize was the no. 1 overall pick, which means he's going to be inserted into a major-league rotation at some point. He features a mid-90s fastball along with a very mature split-finger that kept SEC hitters honest for three years when he twirled the pitch at Auburn (including a no-hitter last year). Along with a retooled slider and newly-discovered cut fastball, he commands all four pitches with maturity. After Auburn was eliminated in the NCAA super regionals, he had amassed well over 110 innings, so after a taste of Single-A he'll go into his first full season learning all those life lessons that one does in professional baseball, such as: sometimes you don't pitch on Friday, and also there's no homework due the next day. Getting money for baseball rules!

YEAR	TEAM	LVL	AGE	WHIP	ERA	DRA	WARP	MPH	FB%	WHF	CSP
2018	LAK	A+	21	1.29	4.63	4.44	0.1				
2019	DET	MLB	22	1.44	5.05	5.28	0.1				

Franklin Perez   RHP

Born: 12/06/97   Age: 21   Bats: R   Throws: R
Height: 6'3"   Weight: 197   Origin: International Free Agent, 2014

YEAR	TEAM	LVL	AGE	W	L	SV	G	GS	IP	H	HR	BB/9	K/9	K	GB%	BABIP
2016	QUD	A	18	3	3	1	15	10	66²	63	1	2.6	10.1	75	39%	.344
2017	BCA	A+	19	4	2	2	12	10	54¹	38	4	2.7	8.8	53	38%	.236
2017	CCH	AA	19	2	1	1	7	6	32	33	2	3.1	7.0	25	35%	.316
2018	LAK	A+	20	0	1	0	4	4	11¹	15	2	6.4	7.1	9	43%	.371
2019	DET	MLB	21	2	2	0	13	6	33	36	5	3.9	6.6	24	37%	.301

Breakout: 1%   Improve: 3%   Collapse: 0%   Attrition: 5%   MLB: 7%
Comparables: Jake Odorizzi, Matt Magill, Homer Bailey

There's still tons of potential in Perez, the centerpiece of the Justin Verlander trade. Worst-case scenario, we're copying and pasting this lead sentence into his next few *Annual* comments, because last year was all but lost for the young flamethrowing starter, from a three-month lat injury to a season-ending shoulder strain. We've yet to see a full workload, but he should impress with his above-average three pitches, the *coup de grace* being the changeup. Double-A is calling, and we'll see if he can stay on the line for a full season.

YEAR	TEAM	LVL	AGE	WHIP	ERA	DRA	WARP	MPH	FB%	WHF	CSP
2016	QUD	A	18	1.23	2.84	3.40	1.2				
2017	BCA	A+	19	0.99	2.98	3.49	1.1				
2017	CCH	AA	19	1.38	3.09	3.51	0.6				
2018	LAK	A+	20	2.03	7.94	5.38	0.0				
2019	DET	MLB	21	1.54	5.36	5.62	-0.2				

LINEOUTS

Hitters

HITTER	POS	TEAM	LVL	AGE	PA	R	2B	3B	HR	RBI	BB	K	SB	CS	AVG/OBP/SLG	DRC+	WARP
Sergio Alcantara	SS	ERI	AA	21	494	53	18	3	1	37	42	95	8	5	.271/.335/.333	89	0.3
Jose Azocar	OF	WMI	A	22	110	19	3	6	1	16	5	21	6	2	.317/.355/.490	129	0.6
	OF	LAK	A+	22	318	34	14	3	1	34	9	64	5	2	.290/.308/.367	107	0.0
Gordon Beckham	2B	TAC	AAA	31	425	64	24	1	10	51	57	52	6	2	.302/.400/.458	128	2.5
	2B	SEA	MLB	31	50	3	1	0	0	1	4	11	1	0	.182/.250/.205	82	0.3
Willi Castro	SS	AKR	AA	21	410	55	20	2	5	39	28	84	13	4	.245/.303/.350	96	1.9
	SS	ERI	AA	21	114	12	9	2	4	13	6	25	4	1	.324/.366/.562	95	0.1
Kody Clemens	2B	WMI	A	22	174	18	10	2	4	17	21	27	3	1	.302/.387/.477	140	0.8
	2B	LAK	A+	22	46	6	2	0	1	3	2	12	1	0	.238/.283/.357	66	-0.1
Brock Deatherage	CF	WMI	A	22	195	25	7	5	2	18	14	50	15	3	.313/.369/.443	117	1.4
	CF	LAK	A+	22	52	12	1	1	1	5	6	13	4	0	.333/.404/.467	108	0.1
Pete Kozma	SS	TOL	AAA	30	296	23	18	2	1	17	19	52	6	1	.203/.260/.295	61	-0.6
	SS	DET	MLB	30	73	7	4	1	1	8	2	15	0	1	.217/.236/.348	80	0.2
Kingston Liniak	OF	TGR	Rk	18	166	14	7	0	0	9	7	51	5	4	.224/.259/.269	46	0.3
	OF	TGW	Rk	18	34	5	1	0	0	4	0	7	2	0	.281/.324/.313	46	0.0
Reynaldo Rivera	1B	WMI	A	21	454	41	28	4	9	62	36	119	3	2	.237/.295/.390	85	-0.9
Jake Robson	OF	ERI	AA	23	311	46	16	3	7	32	39	78	11	4	.286/.382/.450	125	1.5
	OF	TOL	AAA	23	245	36	13	1	4	15	23	62	7	6	.305/.369/.427	120	0.9
Bobby Wilson	C	ROC	AAA	35	45	2	1	0	0	3	3	13	0	0	.125/.182/.150	28	-0.2
	C	MIN	MLB	35	151	12	8	0	2	16	12	37	0	0	.178/.242/.281	66	0.4

Scrawny infielder **Sergio Alcantara** doesn't have the frame or the bat for a starting shortstop gig in his future, but his plus speed, range and pitch recognition will make him a useful bench contributor in a few orbital revolutions. ☉ Free-swinging **Jose Azocar** sputtered in High-A and took an unscheduled detour back a level before getting his GPS coordinates right to hit .330 in his second chance in Florida. ☉ In a new tradition, the Mariners have taken to holding **Gordon Beckham** up to the big league roster every July 1st. If he runs back to Tacoma and hides it's six more weeks of contention. If not, well... ☉ **Willi Castro** is a fringy middle-infield prospect playing beyond his age bracket with the promise of some power, which is why the Indians deemed him expendable in exchange for Leonys Martin. ☉ The fourth and youngest Clemens progeny, **Kody Clemens** is already pigeonholed at second base but finished last season at High-A, so we'll quickly find out who gets to be the second-most-valuable Clemens. ☉ The most metal of prospect names, speedy outfielder **Brock Deatherage** leapt into the mosh pit of professional baseball, thrashed three dingers in his first game and was carried all the way up to High-A. Ooh wa ah ah ah. ☉ **Pete Kozma** keeps showing the youngsters in Triple-A how to play an elite defense, then in return the kids show *him* how to hit for power. The kids then get the call-up instead of him. ⓧ San Diego-area high schooler **Kingston Liniak** took the money and ran with the Tigers as a fourth-round pick. As is the case with young, toolsy high schoolers, he'll get all the time in the world to develop before the sun devours us all. ⓧ Geraldo Rivera looked in Al Capone's vault in search of treasure and left us all disappointed. **Reynaldo Rivera** will spend the next few years trying to tap into his mysterious vault of raw power, though untelevised. ⓧ They call **Jacob Robson** "Maple Hammer" because he is Canadian, but while "Hammer" seems anachronous for a 5-foot-10 outfielder, he's been quickly nailing every minor-league rung since the 2016 draft and may warrant a major-league appearance this year. ⓧ Okay, *now* we've likely seen the last of the longest name in sports, **Jarrod Saltalamacchia**, who mentored battery-mates for a Triple-A summer and was rewarded with one last September as a third catcher. ⓧ **Bobby Wilson** has never been even remotely close to average at the plate, so the fact that he just completed the 16th year of his professional career says a great deal about how teams value his work behind it.

Pitchers

PITCHER	TEAM	LVL	AGE	W	L	SV	G	GS	IP	H	HR	BB/9	K/9	K	GB%	WHIP	ERA	DRA	WARP
Tyler Alexander	ERI	AA	23	3	2	0	9	9	48	64	7	1.7	6.6	35	45%	1.52	3.75	3.91	0.8
	TOL	AAA	23	3	6	0	17	15	92	120	9	1.3	5.9	60	47%	1.45	4.79	4.22	1.4
Ryan Carpenter	DET	MLB	27	1	2	0	6	5	22¹	34	8	1.6	6.0	15	35%	1.70	7.25	5.82	-0.1
	TOL	AAA	27	2	8	0	14	14	76¹	96	8	2.5	8.6	73	35%	1.53	5.07	4.27	1.1
Jose Fernandez	NHP	AA	25	3	1	2	23	0	31¹	23	5	6.6	9.5	33	28%	1.47	3.45	7.22	-0.8
	BUF	AAA	25	1	2	2	21	0	29¹	23	2	2.5	9.8	32	48%	1.06	2.45	2.92	0.7
	TOR	MLB	25	0	0	0	13	0	10¹	10	2	3.5	5.2	6	34%	1.35	6.10	5.76	-0.1
Matt Hall	ERI	AA	24	5	2	0	27	4	57	33	1	3.9	12.0	76	54%	1.02	1.58	2.92	1.4
	TOL	AAA	24	4	0	0	10	10	57¹	46	1	3.1	9.3	59	44%	1.15	2.67	3.90	1.1
	DET	MLB	24	0	0	0	5	0	8	19	1	3.4	5.6	5	51%	2.75	14.62	5.99	-0.1
Zac Houston	ERI	AA	23	1	1	0	13	0	17¹	8	1	4.7	13.0	25	40%	0.98	2.60	2.35	0.5
	TOL	AAA	23	0	1	10	33	0	38	20	2	3.8	13.0	55	48%	0.95	1.18	2.21	1.3
Eduardo Jimenez	LAK	A+	23	3	4	15	40	0	50	62	3	3.6	9.2	51	44%	1.64	3.42	3.06	1.1
Eduardo Paredes	ANA	MLB	23	0	0	0	14	0	18¹	25	5	3.4	7.4	15	41%	1.75	6.87	6.27	-0.3
	SLC	AAA	23	2	1	5	38	0	42¹	44	5	4.0	7.4	35	35%	1.49	4.68	7.15	-1.0
Zac Reininger	TOL	AAA	25	5	1	6	37	0	51¹	46	3	2.8	9.3	53	34%	1.21	2.63	4.43	0.4
	DET	MLB	25	1	0	0	18	0	21¹	28	5	3.8	7.6	18	40%	1.73	7.59	4.71	0.1
Logan Shore	STO	A+	23	2	0	0	4	4	22¹	18	0	0.8	10.1	25	63%	0.90	1.21	4.24	0.3
	MID	AA	23	1	6	0	13	13	68²	85	7	2.5	6.4	49	50%	1.51	5.50	4.81	0.4
Gregory Soto	LAK	A+	23	8	8	0	25	23	113¹	101	4	5.6	9.1	115	47%	1.51	4.45	4.00	1.7

Drafted by the Tigers in 2013 and then again in 2015, **Tyler Alexander** has modest potential as a back-end starter and figures to make his big-league debut in 2019. ⑨ Spaghetti western villain/Triple-A reliever **Johnny Barbato** added a splitter to go with his fastball-slider revue. Anything to start silencing more bats, all of which currently act like Clint Eastwood protagonists against him. ⑨ Originally the Rays' seventh-round pick in 2011, **Ryan Carpenter** finally made his MLB debut at age 27 as part of the Tigers' clown car of a bullpen. ⑨ Everyone loves a lefty reliever, but **Jose Fernandez** pushed that trope to its natural limit in 2018 as he couldn't control his mid-90s heater and has yet to develop a proper breaking ball. ⑨ **Matt Hall**'s looping curveball won him the Tigers' minor-league pitcher of the year thanks to 21 straight shutout innings as well as a September cameo in the show. With a get-me-over fastball, that's enough for a smattering of innings, at least until Hall takes what's behind pitch no. 3. ⑨ **Zac Houston** is a one-pitch reliever who's demolished wood-based blunt instruments at every level with an enigmatic low-to-mid-90s fastball. He'll almost certainly get a bullpen cameo this year, where he will learn they're called "bats." ⑨ Credit to **Eduardo Jimenez**, who broke the mold of the Tigers' power pitching prospect who can't find the strike zone: he finds too much of it, as lefties hit .347 against him last year. ⑨ Perhaps the nicest thing one can say about **Eduardo Paredes**' 2018 is that he finished .03 shy of 6.90 ERA. ⑨ **Zac Reininger**'s biggest change last year was cutting his long hair because, hey, it worked for Jacob deGrom. The difference is deGrom has about eight different out-pitches, about nine more than Reininger. ⑨ Aussie hurler **Warwick Saupold** profiles better as a starter given his pitch-to-contact approach, but he was given the ol' didgeridoo off the roster last year (that means outrighted in "Australian," probably). ⑨ **Logan Shore** has been hampered by injuries and lack of stuff since being drafted out of the University of Florida in the second round in 2016. His upside is probably Mike Fiers, for whom he was traded as a PTBNL last year. ⑨ It might be time for lefty starter **Gregory Soto** to see what his fastball can do in the bullpen, because if he remains a starter he might occasionally get called "Gregory Soso" and nobody can recover from a burn like that.

Tigers Prospects

The State of the System:

Dave Dombrowksi may be celebrating a World Series back east, but the rebuilding Tigers still have a whole bunch of right-handed pitching prospects.

The Top Ten:

1

Casey Mize   RHP   OFP: 60   Likely: 55   ETA: Late 2019
Born: 05/01/97   Age: 22   Bats: R   Throws: R   Height: 6'3"   Weight: 220
Origin: Round 1, 2018 Draft (#1 overall)

The Report: Mize is the first college arm to go 1.1 since Mark Appel. Like Appel, he is more of a surety over upside pick. That's not to poo-poo the stuff here. Mize has three potential plus pitches in his fastball/slider/split combo. The fastball sits comfortably mid-90s and Mize attacks the zone with it to set up his power slider and split-change. The slider has mid-80s velocity and good two-plane break, and his split has big velo separation and plenty of tumble. The Tigers have taken a fairly conservative path with him so far—he had some injury issues his sophomore year—but he could debut next year and I'd expect him to start in the Eastern League. There is some effort in his delivery to note. The mechanics are extremely arm-heavy and he will whack and recoil at times. It remains to be seen whether that will work across a starter's workload in the pros. Regardless, he's essentially major-league-ready now, which was the argument for him as the first overall pick as opposed to a huge projection or ceiling.

The Risks: Medium. Mize could probably be dropped into a rotation Opening Day and be at least average. That won't happen for the obvious reasons. He has had arm issues in college and is a pitching prospect so there's always that.

Ben Carsley's Fantasy Take: It's not Mize's fault that he went 1.1, but because of his draft slot he's nearly guaranteed to be overrated in dynasty circles. Reading up on Mize above, he profiles similarly to how Kyle Wright did coming into 2018, whom we ranked at 81 on our top-101 before last season. Such a ranking for Mize might seem harsh, but is more indicative of the risk-to-reward ratio that comes with any mid-rotation starting pitching prospect than any real flaw on Mize's part.

2

Matt Manning RHP   OFP: 60   Likely: 50   ETA: 2020
Born: 01/28/98   Age: 21   Bats: R   Throws: R   Height: 6'6"   Weight: 190
Origin: Round 1, 2016 Draft (#9 overall)

The Report: Manning looked more like the ninth overall pick in 2018. He's now sitting in the mid-90s and sawing off hitters with the heater's natural cutter-like action. His curveball is getting sharper, too. It isn't consistently plus, but he's flashing the best version of it more and more. Manning still has quite a few flaws in his profile, though. He's cleaned up his mechanics somewhat, and his command has improved accordingly, but he doesn't take full advantage of his size. His back knee collapses as he begins his stride, which limits the plane his 6-foot-6 frame can provide. More importantly, he hasn't settled on a changeup that works for him. Detroit has him working with a fosh for now, but that may change. There's still plenty of time for Manning to reach his high ceiling and he'll likely spend 2019 in Double-A as a 21-year old. It isn't difficult to envision him as one of the top prospects in the game a year from now, but...

The Risks: ...it could also quickly go the other way. You don't have to squint very hard to see why people get squirmy projecting him as a starter. Despite tinkering with several grips, he has yet to find a consistently usable changeup. Pair that with spotty command and you've got reliever risk written all over him.

Ben Carsley's Fantasy Take: If you subscribe to the theory that the only thing that matters with pitching prospects is upside, you may actually prefer Manning to Mize. I won't go that far given all the red flags, but I am intrigued by Manning's ceiling as a high-K fantasy SP4/5. That his floor appears to be as a bullpen arm matters, though, and it will be tough for Manning to crack the back of the top-101 dynasty list despite his proximity to the majors.

3

Isaac Paredes IF   OFP: 55   Likely: 50   ETA: Early 2020
Born: 02/18/99   Age: 20   Bats: R   Throws: R   Height: 5'11"   Weight: 225
Origin: International Free Agent, 2015

The Report: Performance-wise Paredes' season was an unqualified success: He reached Double-A as a 19-year-old and had the best overall offensive season of his career. We mostly exist to qualify here though. Although Paredes was the youngest player at his levels, he's not exactly projectable at this point—see the listed height/weight above for one—and those thighs portend a below-average runner in his twenties. He's an aggressive hitter with some length to his swing, but his bat speed/control are sufficient to smooth the edges enough to project at least an average hit tool.

The fire hydrant physique belies above-average raw power, and Paredes should get to enough of it to be a 15-20 home run guy. He's not gonna be rangey enough for shortstop or perhaps even second, but he has plenty of arm for third and the hands and actions to be at least average there. He may retain enough defensive flexibility to play three spots in the infield if you want to spot someone once a week as well. Paredes' profile lacks upside on the scouting sheet—averagish tools across the board and a corner infield projection—but this is also the type of profile (and physique) that seems to pop (so to speak) in the majors these days.

The Risks: Medium. It's more of an all-around profile than a standout, toolsy one, and he's only played a handful of games in the upper minors.

Ben Carsley's Fantasy Take: I feel personally attacked by the description of Paredes' thighs. Anyway, Eduardo Escobar just hit .272 with 23 homers and decent R/RBI stats, and that well-roundedness was enough to make him a top-20 third baseman, per ESPN's player rater. That's the dream with Paredes, who I don't think is on a lot of dynasty radars right now and who could very well be available in your league.

4 **Daz Cameron OF**   OFP: 55   Likely: 50   ETA: Late 2019
Born: 01/15/97   Age: 22   Bats: R   Throws: R   Height: 6'2"   Weight: 195
Origin: Round 1, 2015 Draft (#37 overall)

The Report: Cameron is a tricky guy to project, and Jeff begged off the blurb because he said that it was "breaking his brain." I can see why. Cameron is constantly evolving, which makes it difficult to get a bead on him. With an athletic build and plenty of tools, he checked all the boxes but never performed to potential in Houston's system. A year-and-a-half later, he looks like a major leaguer. He's an above-average hitter with average raw power, but the gap between those two could narrow sooner rather than later. He's a plus runner on the bases and in the field. Cameron is built for center field, but he has enough of an arm that he could play right if that becomes necessary. In the end, his role will be determined by how his bat plays against major-league arms. It won't take much more polish to turn him into a glove-first fourth outfielder, but with a little more power and consistency of contact, he'll be a well-rounded, every day guy.

The Risks: Low. He's close to the majors, handled a halfish season of Double-A well, and has a fairly safe floor as a bench outfielder due to the glove, speed, and arm. Like Paredes there is some positive variance here too if more power comes.

Ben Carsley's Fantasy Take: Cameron is one of the toughest guys in the minors to project from a dynasty standpoint, too. His floor seems to be a faster version of Jackie Bradley Jr., and we've seen JBJ serve as an OF4/5 during his best years. But it's always scary when the hit tool is the biggest question mark with any prospect with this profile. I think Cameron's upside and proximity should push him into top-101 territory, but odds are I won't feel great about the placement. I also wouldn't feel great about leaving him off. Ugh, my brain is broken as well.

5 **Beau Burrows   RHP**   OFP: 55   Likely: 50   ETA: Late 2019
Born: 09/18/96   Age: 22   Bats: R   Throws: R   Height: 6'2"   Weight: 200
Origin: Round 1, 2015 Draft (#22 overall)

The Report: Burrows followed up his successful 2017 campaign with a full season in Double-A that ultimately raised more questions than answers. The plus heater was a couple ticks down all year, sitting 91-94 instead of the 93-96. His changeup is still his most advanced secondary, and the excellent velo separation and arm speed are enough to project it as an above-average future offering despite average movement. His 12-6 curve flashes plus too, but the inconsistency in its movement and an overall lack of command causes it to play half a grade down.

Three above-average future offerings is all good and well, but Burrows has yet to make the necessary command refinements in order to get the most out of his stuff. He struck out less than a batter per inning and walked almost four per nine this season. His mechanics are clean and he repeats well though, so the command may just be what it is at this point. The quality of his pitch mix will always leave you wanting more, but this is still a 21-year-old former first rounder who just spent the season in Double-A. Burrows may never develop into the mid-rotation arm many thought he would, but he projects as a solid fourth starter who should begin 2019 in Triple-A.

The Risks: Moderate. Burrows does throw baseballs for a living but unless the command regresses at the big-league level, he's a probable rotation piece with the upside for more.

Ben Carsley's Fantasy Take: Burrows just doesn't miss enough bats for us to get particularly excited about his fantasy future, especially in an era when strikeouts are at an all-time high. Burrows figures to have his uses in uber-deep leagues or AL-only formats, but for those of you who play in standard keeper/dynasty leagues with 100-150ish prospects owned, he's an afterthought at present.

6 **Franklin Perez   RHP**   OFP: 60   Likely: 45   ETA: 2020
Born: 12/06/97   Age: 21   Bats: R   Throws: R   Height: 6'3"   Weight: 197
Origin: International Free Agent, 2014

The Report: The 2018 report on Perez is actually an HMO explanation of benefits. A lat strain last spring cost him the first half of the season, and shoulder irritation shut him down in the second half after ~20 mostly ineffective innings. This comes a year after a knee issue that kept him under 100 innings in 2017. We know what he is capable of when healthy—a heavy fastball that touches 96, a potential plus curve and change—but we are going to need to see it for a full season on the mound… at some point. On the one hand he is still 21 for a few more weeks, on the other—well, the phrase "shoulder irritation" basically.

The Risks: High. Perez has never thrown more than 86 1/3 innings in a season due to a variety of maladies. He's only made seven starts above A-ball, and 2018 was a lost developmental year. We have no idea if he can handle a real workload.

Ben Carsley's Fantasy Take: Despite the massive risks, I prefer Perez to Burrows from a fantasy perspective. Sure, he's got greater odds of flaming out or moving to the pen, but if he does stay on the mound for significant periods of time, he's likely to miss plenty of bats while doing so. He's one for the watch list if he's been dropped in your league, as there's SP5/6 upside here.

7 **Alex Faedo   RHP** OFP: 55   Likely: 45   ETA: 2020
Born: 11/12/95   Age: 23   Bats: R   Throws: R   Height: 6'5"   Weight: 230
Origin: Round 1, 2017 Draft (#18 overall)

The Report: Faedo is not exactly the same pitcher who was a 1.1 candidate going into the 2017 season. He's lost a few ticks off the fastball now and works either side of 90. The slider is still potentially a plus offering, but now comes in only a bit slower than the fastball. Faedo also features an average change with sink and fade in the low-80s. It's now an averageish repertoire tied together by plus command. Faedo has a solid frame and efficient delivery, but the stuff is now more back-of-the-rotation.

The Risks: Medium. Despite the stuff not popping like it did at U of F, Faedo has had pro success due to his command and secondaries. Although unlikely at this point, there's also some positive variance in play if the mid-90s velo returns.

Ben Carsley's Fantasy Take: Faedo was a popular sleeper pick among newly eligible dynasty league prospects last offseason, but the velo drop and corresponding drop in ceiling are big deals for us. If you look at the report and not the name value/draft position, there's little that distinguishes Faedo from lots of guys with similar profiles. He's like a riskier Burrows who's also another year away.

8 **Jake Rogers   C** OFP: 50   Likely: 45   ETA: Late 2019
Born: 04/18/95   Age: 24   Bats: R   Throws: R   Height: 6'1"   Weight: 190
Origin: Round 3, 2016 Draft (#97 overall)

The Report: You aren't going to find a better defensive catching prospect than Rogers. Nimble and athletic behind the dish, he's a fantastic receiver with a plus arm that plays even better due to one of the quickest releases you'll ever see. His defense has been big-league ready for several years now and Rogers clubbed 17 homers for Double-A Erie this season, practically ensuring he'll reach the majors in some capacity.

So, what's the catch? Well, Rogers has extreme bat-to-ball issues and he struck out in 27.5% of his plate appearances last year. The Tigers have been working with him to tame his leg kick, but the swing is still a bit of a mess. His timing is all over the place and isn't helped in the slightest by his poor breaking ball recognition. His bat control is well below-average too, and pitchers often exploit him on the outside part of the plate. Rogers does work the count and he walked in more than 10 percent of his plate appearances for the third season running. Still, quality arms won't be afraid to challenge him in the zone. There's average raw power here, yet it's becoming increasingly unlikely that Rogers can fully realize it in games. Essentially, he's a three true outcomes hitter with below-average game power.

The Risks: Moderate. Usually when a prospect is facing major questions with the stick he's exclusively of the high-risk variety. The defensive package is too good to keep Rogers from a major-league role though, so we'll go with "moderate" here. He's either going to hit enough dongs to profile as a regular or he'll carve out a decade-long career as a defensive-oriented backup.

Ben Carsley's Fantasy Take: Rogers is a great prospect for those of you in 30-team, two-catcher AL Central-only formats.

9

Kyle Funkhouser   RHP   OFP: 50   Likely: 40
ETA: Late 2019, health permitting
Born: 03/16/94   Age: 25   Bats: R   Throws: R   Height: 6'2"   Weight: 220
Origin: Round 4, 2016 Draft (#115 overall)

The Report: In 2018 Funkhouser continued to flash better stuff than he had his senior year and first pro summer, but again he had trouble staying healthy. This year it was a broken foot instead of vague arm issues, which is an improvement of sorts one supposes. Still, Funkhouser will be 25 in March and has yet to complete a full healthy pro season. More maddening is that the stuff remains inconsistent. He'll show mid-90s heat at times, but often works a few ticks lower. He struggles to command the fastball armside, and his control is fringy generally. He'll flash occasional wiggle to back it over the plate gloveside, but the pitch is a bit straight otherwise.

Funkhouser will flash a plus slider with good depth, but the pitch can get a bit lazy/slurvy. His curve rides high too often and doesn't really show good 12-6 action. The change is used sparingly but has a chance to be average. There's some effort in the delivery despite compact arm action. He might be best deployed as a fastball/slider reliever. There's enough here to keep chasing that first round pick people saw his junior season at Louisville, but I haven't really seen it in the pros.

The Risks: Medium. He's been old for his levels and rarely as durable or efficient as you'd like, but the stuff is mostly major-league-ready.

Ben Carsley's Fantasy Take: As a card-carrying member of Weird-Ass Baseball Name Twitter I'm rooting for Funkhouser to succeed. As a dynasty leaguer, I'm staying away.

10 **Carlos Guzman   RHP**   OFP: 50   Likely: 40   ETA: 2022
Born: 05/16/98   Age: 21   Bats: R   Throws: R   Height: 6'1"   Weight: 170
Origin: International Free Agent, 2015

The Report: Guzman spent his first two professional seasons as an infielder before converting to the mound in 2017. Given his lack of pitching experience, the present arsenal is impressive. His low-90s fastball comes out easy and features wicked armside run that you can't teach. His velocity was inconsistent this season. He touched 95 at times, but also had starts where he sat 89-92. There's projection left in his frame though, and his mechanics are free and easy, so I wouldn't be shocked if he's a 92-95 guy with more reps and physical development.

The change is his best secondary currently, which is unusual for a position player convert. It flashes plus in the low-80s with fade and sink. Guzman is confident enough to throw it at any time and to both righties and lefties, although again, it could be an inconsistent offering. The breaking ball, a slurvy high-70s slider, lags behind; he tends to guide the pitch and snap it off. This ranking is very much a projection bet based on Guzman's frame, present stuff, and general athleticism, but the present stuff is better than you'd expect given his background.

The Risks: Extreme. He's a recent pitching convert with only a short-season resume and questions about his durability and breaking ball.

Ben Carsley's Fantasy Take: You know the look I'm giving you.

The Next Five:

11 **Christin Stewart   OF**
Born: 12/10/93   Age: 25   Bats: L   Throws: R   Height: 6'0"   Weight: 205
Origin: Round 1, 2015 Draft (#34 overall)

Stewart cut down on the whiffs in 2018, but gave back a bit of his prodigious pop to do it. The overall profile hasn't changed much. He's better suited to DH than play corner OF—fortunately the Tigers have an opening there for 2019—and the bat might end up less than ideal for your designated masher. Still, a guy who hits .260 with 25 bombs has his uses on a second division team, which the Tigers look to be for a bit, and he can occasionally rotate out to 1B or LF and not kill. You may need to platoon him, and if the swing-and-miss issues creep back in against major-league pitching, the bottom drops out of this profile quickly.

12 **Parker Meadows   OF**
Born: 11/02/99   Age: 19   Bats: L   Throws: R   Height: 6'5"   Weight: 185
Origin: Round 2, 2018 Draft (#44 overall)

The Tigers used their savings at 1.1 to go significantly overslot for Meadows, younger brother of Austin. Parker is even longer and leaner than his older sibling. He's a borderline plus-plus runner and a good bet to stick in center field even as the frame fills out. The offensive profile will require a bit more projection. More power may come in time, as Meadows is currently short to the ball without much in the way of lift. Well, short to the ball once he starts to swing. There's a hand dip which could affect his timing against better velocity. There's clearly the starter kit for a major-league center fielder here, but it may take a while, and a fourth outfielder projection always lurks in the shadows of these profiles.

13 Elvin Rodriguez   RHP
Born: 03/31/98   Age: 21   Bats: R   Throws: R   Height: 6'3"   Weight: 160
Origin: International Free Agent, 2014

The Tigers took on a long-term project when they acquired this skinny righty from the Angels. Rodriguez's three-pitch mix won't blow anyone away, but his consistently solid performances have earned him a spot on the radar. His fastball, which comes in at 89-93, is effective in every part of the zone when he has his best command. It's reasonable to believe that the heater will get a tick better as he matures and adds muscle to his thin frame. Rodriguez also throws a curveball, his most consistently above-average pitch. He does a good job of keeping it low in the zone and preventing solid contact. His changeup is also projectable and he has more confidence in it than many minor leaguers do. He maintains his arm speed on the pitch and it looks like a fastball before fading below the zone. All three pitches flash above-average. They aren't quite there yet, though, and that puts extra pressure on his command. There's little margin for error here, but Rodriguez could be a backend starter when all is said and done.

14 Wenceel Perez   SS
Born: 10/30/99   Age: 19   Bats: B   Throws: R   Height: 5'11"   Weight: 170
Origin: International Free Agent, 2016

Perez has bat-to-ball ability that rivals any player in the low minors. He has a knack for contact and he'll likely add strength as he matures. A little extra power could excuse some of his poorer choices when it comes to pitch selection, an area he could stand to improve. That said, he's a bat-first middle infielder with the tools to play everyday if all goes well. His defense is less impressive. He doesn't react as quickly as one would hope and his actions are stiff at times. While his future is on the dirt, he may need to move to second base, which would put more stress on the bat. In any case, it'll be years before we find out.

15 Willi Castro   SS
Born: 04/24/97   Age: 22   Bats: B   Throws: R   Height: 6'1"   Weight: 165
Origin: International Free Agent, 2013

I was half-tempted to do the Spiderman-pointing-at-himself meme here with Dixon Machado and Willi Castro's faces photoshopped on the webcrawlers', but of course Ben Carsley already beat me to the gag. That's also a bit unfair to Castro—there's a range of outcomes here from Dixon Machado to, like, Jose Iglesias. Castro is a sure-shot shortstop, a switch-hitter with potentially fringy pop. That makes for a very useful utility infielder even if his aggressive approach gets exploited in the majors.

Others of note:

Kody Clemens, IF, High-A Lakeland

Clemens is a high effort player and an offensively-minded middle infielder. His defensive actions are a bit choppy but his gritty, all-out play compensates for that somewhat. At the plate, Clemens was far more polished than your average Midwest League player. He's poised in the box and has an efficient swing path, strong pitch selection, and enough power to punish misplaced offerings. If things go sour at the keystone, he may still hit enough to make a transition to left a viable option. Impressing in the MWL didn't move the needle much in his favor, though—he only did what he was supposed to do. A full season against better pitchers will provide a better litmus test as to how he'll fare going forward. If he hits next year, he'll be in legitimate contention for a top ten spot, even as the Tigers system continues to improve.

Tarik Skubal, LHP, Full-season-A West Michigan

Just on the stuff Skubal should be up there with the ordinal dudes, arguably even in the Top Ten. Of course, just on the stuff he should never have lasted to the ninth round and should have signed for far more than $350,000. You can probably guess the hanging thread here. Skubal had Tommy John surgery in college, and then struggled some to throw strikes in the WAC this past spring in his first season back. He'll also turn 22 next week. How much does this matter? Well, it makes it more likely he's a reliever, despite potentially having three major-league pitches in his locker. It matters less when he's pumping mid-90s heat down in the zone from the left side, when the breaker has two-plane bite, when the change is showing average tumble and fade. Also, he might just be a really good reliever, and that was always in the cards given the effort in his arm action and the funk in the mechanics. Regardless, I think he's a safe bet to be a 2020 Top Ten Tigers prospect. But of course, he's also not safe at all.

Wilkel Hernandez, RHP, Full-season-A West Michigan

Hernandez was the other live arm the Tigers got in 2017 for Ian Kinsler. I can report that the arm is still very much live in 2018. There's mid-90s heat with good life up, and he can touch higher. It's easy velocity from a classically projectable frame. Hernandez shows some feel for spin and the requisite crude change-up.

Hernandez is athletic, though not always enough to keep his long limbs and herky-jerky mechanics all under control. He's probably a reliever long term. He may never manage to throw enough strikes to get out of A-ball, but it could also come together next year and we'll see him near the top of our 2020 Tigers Prospect List.

Top Talents 25 and Under (born 4/1/93 or later):

1. Casey Mize
2. Matt Manning
3. Isaac Paredes
4. Daz Cameron
5. Jeimer Candelario
6. Beau Burrows
7. Franklin Perez
8. Joe Jimenez
9. Alex Faedo
10. Jake Rogers

Those of you familiar with the state of the Tiger's 25U list will note that Michael Fulmer has finally aged out of it. In his place lies Mize, the No. 1 overall draft pick who should be a fair replacement holder for fans' hopes and dreams. He throws right-handed too so if you miss Fulmer too much, go ahead and just scribble a bushy beard on him in your head.

Candelario's spot was determined with no small amount of hand wringing. Given the variance in defensive metrics, and which ones you choose to place your faith in, he could conceivably slide up or down a spot or two. He probably won't be much more than the competent regular he was last year, but competence is an often underrated skill, and one the Tigers could certainly use more of.

The rest of the big-league squad is much older than a team that just lost 98 games for the second straight season has any sense being. Nick Castellanos is too old for our purposes, and while Daniel Norris continues to exist, he does so only just. Joe Jimenez is an easy punchline, as giving a team's sole All-Star spot to a setup reliever should be a jailable offense, though that's no fault of his. He's a perfectly fine, if non-elite, relief arm with a powerful arsenal and now a full year of major-league success.

After that, this list takes a strong turn for the minors, and you can find plenty of insight on all of these players through the magic of scrolling upwards. Overall, the Tigers are preparing to enter year three of the inevitable dark period that comes from spending to the hilt and leveraging your farm for big-league upgrades at every opportunity. While the best players in this group don't appear to have the superstar ceiling of other organizations, the Tigers are starting to see the results of a commitment to development with a large cache of projectable talent, particularly among their right-handed pitchers. With the addition of last year's 1.1 pick, expect to see Detroit rise in the farm system rankings and, if all goes to plan, the big-league standings come 2020.

Part 3: Featured Articles

The Hole in The Shift is Fixing Itself

Russell Carleton

I've been on a bit of a mission against The Shift of late. I'm not out to get The Shift for the usual reasons that people oppose it. The words "the right way to play the game" won't be found on my lips. If a team wants to pursue a strategy that is within the rules and it works, then by all means, they have my blessing (not that they need it). Instead, my concern with The Shift is a worry that it doesn't work, or at least that it has a flaw that needs fixing.

The data show that while The Shift does a decent job of preventing singles on balls in play (what it's supposed to do), it also increases the number of walks that happen in front of it, and the number of additional walks outweighs the number of singles saved. It's a problem because you can't throw a guy out if he gets to walk to first base.

But the "why" was important. It seemed that The Shift was changing the way in which pitchers pitched. We saw that there were fewer fastballs thrown in front of The Shift than we might otherwise expect, and that pitchers tended to stay out of the strike zone a little more. Not by a lot. In fact, it might not even be visible to the naked eye. The percentage of pitches that are out of the zone goes from 51.0 to 53.3 from a standard defense (two right/two left) to a full shift (three on one side). That difference stands up even after we control for the types of hitters that get shifted against. And it's enough to drive up the walk rate to where it cancels out the benefits that teams thought they were getting with The Shift… and then some.

But there was some hope. I found that when individual pitchers stayed closer to the in-zone/out-of-zone mix that they used without The Shift on, they could still get the benefits of The Shift without the walk problems. So, in theory, a team could simply figure out a way to convince its pitchers to not fall prey to the walk trap and The Shift would once again be their friend.

It's reasonable to think that some teams might be more hip to this idea than others. Maybe some figured it out a year before the others. Maybe they were better at getting the message across to their pitchers. Or, maybe no one has figured it out yet.

Warning! Gory Mathematical Details Ahead!

I used data from 2015-2017, made available through MLB's data portal, Baseball Savant. They are kind enough to note when teams are using an infield shift (three fielders on one side of second base), as opposed to a "strategic shift" (someone's playing a bit out of position, but it's not quite that drastic) or a "standard" alignment.

Since we're doing this by team, I can't just look at raw walk rates, because we know that some teams have good pitchers and others have not-so-good pitchers. Some have a mix of both. I used the log-odds ratio method to take into account a batter's general walking proclivities, and a pitcher's as well, and then shoving them into a binary logistic regression. Then, I asked the computer to generate a specific coefficient for each team's pitchers, for when they went into The Shift and how that affected their walk rate.

Using those coefficients, I was able to project what would happen if a league-average pitcher faced a league-average hitter (which we expect would product a league-average walk rate; from 2015-2017, 7.7 percent of plate appearances ended in a walk) and then just switched his hat. Here's the top five and the bottom five:

Top 5 Teams	Projected Shift Walk Rate	Bottom 5 Teams	Projected Shift Walk Rate
Rockies	6.2%	Rangers	11.2%
Pirates	6.7%	Mets	10.4%
Indians	7.2%	Dodgers	10.2%
Astros	7.3%	Cardinals	9.9%
Braves	7.7%	Tigers	9.7%

There are probably people out there right now trying to figure out what the common thread is among the top and bottom teams. I'm sure, because this is Baseball Prospectus, people are already trying to make the case that sabermetric "early adopters" have some sort of edge here. I think that the more interesting piece is that by the time you get to fifth place in The Shift, we're at league average.

As a sanity check, I examined the issue on a pitch-by-pitch level, looking at how often pitchers threw their pitches in the GameDay strike zone, and again using the same basic methodology and getting team-specific coefficients. The names on the list re-arranged themselves, but the idea was the same, and the two lists correlated with an R of .593.

There's a reason that I don't usually do this type of leaderboard post. I don't really know what the Rockies, Pirates, Indians, Astros, and Braves have in common, or what they have that the bottom five don't. I can put a shrug emoji here and say, "Well, it must be something!" but that seems like a cop-out. Instead, I'd like to present another table and suggest that the table above doesn't even really matter anymore.

Year	League Percent Outside K Zone (Full Shift)	League Percent in K Zone (No Shift)	Difference
2015	54.1%	51.1%	3.0%
2016	53.3%	50.9%	2.4%
2017	52.6%	50.9%	1.7%
2018	52.0%	50.7%	1.3%

The hole in The Shift is fixing itself, and it's coming down really fast league wide. In my earlier work on The Shift, I suggested that until teams stopped having such a huge difference between their out-of-zone rate with and without The Shift on, there would just be too many walks for The Shift to make sense. It seems that all 30 of them have been working toward just that. I once estimated that it takes about 10 years for an idea to filter its way through baseball. At this rate, it looks like teams are going to catch up a lot faster than that. And yeah, they're all saber-smart now.

It's likely that whatever magic it was that the Rockies and Pirates had has made its way to Texas and Queens. Or is at least on its way. And if teams are committing to fixing the walk problem, then it's likely that they will continue shifting and shifting a lot.

And eventually it's going to actually make sense for them to do it.

—Russell Carleton is a former author of Baseball Prospectus and now an analyst for the New York Mets.

The State of the Quality Start

Rob Mains

O ne of the seven things you (probably) didn't know about the 2018 season is that quality starts—defined as a start lasting six or more innings with three or fewer earned runs allowed—as a percentage of total starts cratered to an all-time low of 41 percent. I want to look a little more deeply into this, since it's been a while (May of 2016, to be exact) since I've examined quality starts.

The term *quality start* is credited to *Philadelphia Inquirer* sportswriter John Lowe. It's been derided ever since he coined it in December of 1985. Three runs in six innings? That's a 4.50 ERA! In what world is that a measure of quality?

Let's start with that criticism. It's true that 3 x 9 / 6 = 4.5. (You came here for this sort of high-level math, right?) But it's also true that type of start, meeting the bare minimum for earning a quality start, is unusual. Here's the proportion of quality starts in which the pitcher lasted exactly six innings and yielded exactly three earned runs. (I'm going to confine this analysis to the 30-team era, 1998-present. Almost all data retrieved in this article is via the Baseball-Reference Play Index.)

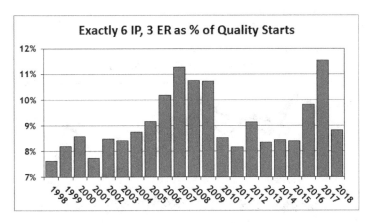

There were 1,997 quality starts in 2018. Only 176, or fewer than one in 11, featured a pitcher going six innings and allowing three earned runs. Put another way, the percentage of quality starts that resulted in a 4.50 ERA (8.8 percent) is less than half the percentage of games in which a batter hit two home runs and his team lost (22.5 percent; 237-69 won-lost). That doesn't impugn hitting two homers.

So if a 4.50 ERA isn't the norm, what is? How good are quality starts?

Pretty good, it turns out. First, on a team level:

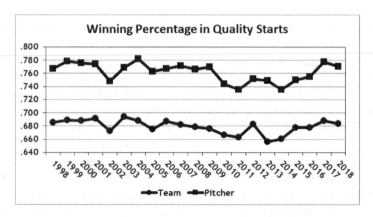

Teams receiving a quality start from their pitcher won 68.4 percent of their games in 2018, in line with the 30-team era average of 67.9 percent. A team with a .684 winning percentage wins 111 games. Getting a quality start is definitely a good thing. Individual pitchers throwing quality starts have a higher winning percentage because a big slice of team losses is assigned to a reliever.

If teams do well in quality starts, how well do the starting pitchers do? Again, very well.

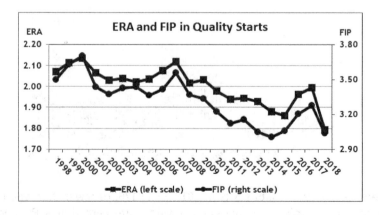

Pitchers in quality starts had a 1.79 ERA (blue line) in 2018, *the lowest in the 30-team era*. Their FIP was higher, 3.04, but still excellent. In the 30-team era, only 2014 had a lower FIP for quality starts, 3.01.

But, of course, the run environment in 2014 was different. Teams in 2014 scored 4.07 runs per game, the fewest in a non-strike year since 1976. They scored 4.45 runs per game in 2018. So surrendering a 3.04 FIP in 2018 is more impressive than 3.01 in 2014. Accordingly, let's look at ERA and FIP in quality starts relative to league averages.

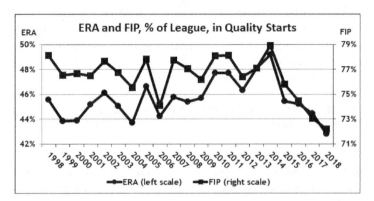

This tells a more dramatic story. Starting pitchers in 2018 gave up a 4.19 ERA and a 4.21 FIP. Starters in quality starts gave up a 1.79 ERA, 43 percent of the league average. Starters in quality starts gave up a 3.04 FIP, 72 percent of the league average. Both of these marks represent lows in the 30-team era.

The takeaway here is this: *Quality starts are better, relative to other starts, than they've ever been over the past 21 years.*

Maybe during the winter I'll look at this over a longer arc of time. For now, though, we can definitively say quality starts are the best they've ever been since the Diamondbacks and Rays joined the majors.

Yet, paradoxically, they're down.

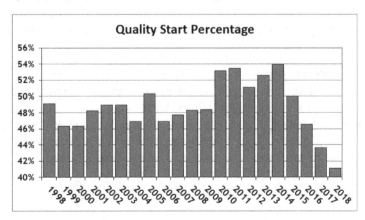

This graph covers only the 30-team era. In my article last week, though, I looked at the years 1908-2018. The result was the same. The 41 percent of starts in 2018 that were quality starts are an all-time low, well below the runners-up: 1930's 43 percent (the year teams scored an all-time record 5.55 runs per game) and last year's 44 percent.

The normal explanation for a dip in quality start percentage is an increase in scoring. When teams score a lot of runs, it's harder for starting pitchers to last six or more innings and limit opponents to three earned runs. From 1998 to 2014, the correlation between runs scored per game and the percentage of starts that were quality starts was -0.94. That means there was an extremely close relationship: More runs, fewer quality starts. Too small a sample? Go back to the start of the Expansion Era, 1961, and the relationship is even more negative, a -0.95 correlation, though 2014.

But that's broken down over the past four years:

- 2015: Runs per game increased from 4.07 to 4.25, quality start percentage decreased from 54.0 to 50.1. Yes, that's a negative relationship, but the regression model would predict a decline of 1.5 percentage points. We got 3.9 instead.

- 2016: Runs per game increased from 4.25 to 4.48, quality start percentage decreased from 50.1 to 46.6. Past experience would suggest a decline of just 1.8 percentage points. We got 3.4.

- 2017: Runs per game increased from 4.48 to 4.65, quality start percentage decreased from 46.6 to 43.6. Again, the direction's right, but the magnitude isn't. Using the relationship from 1998 to 2014, that increase in scoring should've reduced quality starts by 1.3 percentage points, not 2.9.

- 2018: Runs per game declined from 4.65 to 4.45. That should've resulted in the quality start percentage moving in the other direction, rising 1.6 points. It didn't. It fell 2.6 points, as noted, to an all-time low.

Granted, we're talking about just four years here. Maybe they're outliers. But I don't think they are. Quality starts, as noted, are as good or better than ever. But they're rarer than ever as well. And I think I know why.

To get a quality start, you need to allow three or fewer earned and pitch at least six innings. That's 18 outs. Here's a graph showing the number of starting pitchers who limited their opponents to three or fewer earned runs but got pulled after pitching at least five innings but fewer than six:

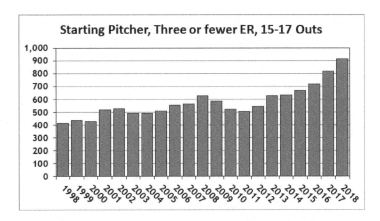

A pitcher getting 15 outs pitched five innings. A pitcher getting 16 outs pitched 5 1/3. A pitcher getting 17 outs pitched 5 2/3. More than ever before, pitchers are being removed from games in which they are within 1-3 outs of a quality start, falling just short of the six-inning finish line. Widespread acknowledgement of the times-through-the-order penalty and a flotilla of available bullpen arms is making the quality start simultaneously both more excellent and more rare.

Which is ironic, given that we saw a new post-war quality start record this season:

Rank	Pitcher	Season	Consecutive QS
1	Jacob deGrom	2018	24
2	Bob Gibson	1968	22
-	Chris Carpenter	2005	22
4	Johan Santana	2004	21
5	Luis Tiant	1968	20
-	Mike Scott	1986	20
-	Jake Arrieta	2015	20
8	Robin Roberts	1952	19
-	Tom Seaver	1973	19
-	Jack Morris	1983	19
-	Greg Maddux	1998	19
-	Josh Johnson	2010	19
-	Jon Lester	2014	19

While there have been longer streaks spread over multiple seasons, no pitcher since World War II threw more consecutive quality starts in one year than Jacob deGrom this year. The fact that he did in a year in which quality starts were the rarest they've ever been adds to the accomplishment. ▓

—Rob Mains is an author of Baseball Prospectus.

Heads-Up Hacking—The First Pitch

Matthew Trueblood

Batters fell behind in a higher percentage of all plate appearances in 2018 than in any previous season for which we have pitch-by-pitch data. That kind of granular information goes back only to 1988, but we might safely assume (given all we know about baseball as it had been before that, and as it has been in the years since) that batters have *never* fallen behind at a higher rate than they did last season.

Through the 1990s, the percentage of all plate appearances that began 0-1 hovered in the high 30s and low 40s. In the 2000s, it rose steadily but slowly, through the mid-40s. In 2018, 49.8 percent of all trips to the plate began 0-1. That, as much as anything, captures in microcosm the nature of hitting in MLB today.

A countdown clock toward strike three begins ticking almost the moment a batter takes his place in the box. The league's adjusted OPS+ on the first pitch was higher in 2018 than ever before, and that has been true in most of the last 10 seasons. Batters hit .264/.289/.442 in all plate appearances in which they swung at the first pitch last season, and .241/.330/.395 in all plate appearances in which they took that first offering.

The percentage differences in batting average and isolated power there favor swinging at the first pitch by more than in any season since 1988, while the difference in on-base percentage favors taking by more than ever. If you want to get on base at a decent clip, it's a good idea to be patient, but you run the risk of missing the only chances you'll get to produce power.

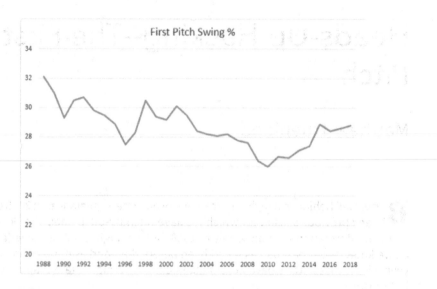

First Pitch Swing %

The league swung at the first pitch 28.8 percent of the time in 2018. With the isolated exception of 2015, that's the highest that number has climbed since 2002, but it might not be high enough. With the help of BP research maven Rob McQuown, I looked at the aggregate Called Strike Probability (CSProb) on the first pitch for each season since 2008, when the implementation of PITCHf/x first made measuring that possible. It's risen sharply during that period.

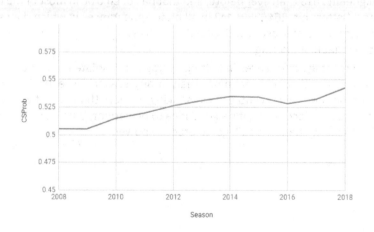

Called Strike Probability, First Pitch of PA (2008-2018)

Called Strike Probability is exactly what it sounds like: a pitch with a given CSProb has roughly that chance of being called a strike, if not swung at. In 2018, a batter who took 100 first pitches from a random sampling of the league's pitchers might expect to fall behind 54 or 55 times—up from 50 or 51 times in 2008. Almost regardless of pitch type (and, notably, especially in the case of fastballs), the first pitch tends to have more of the zone right now than ever before.

Pitchers are better at throwing strikes. They have better stuff, and believe more in their ability to miss bats within the zone. Perhaps most importantly, they know that batters are looking for one thing on the first pitch: a fastball. If they don't get it, they're likely to take the pitch. Check out how the use of sinkers and four-seamers on the first pitch has changed in a decade:

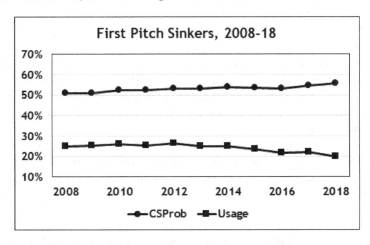

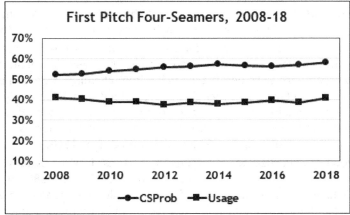

The sinker is losing its place in baseball, but the rate at which pitchers have thrown it on the first pitch hasn't dropped any faster than its usage rate in other counts. Pitchers have actually gone to their four-seamer *more* often to open counts, in the last few years, after a dip in the 2012-2015 period. What's really changed, though, and what shows up in both charts above, is that pitchers are catching more of the zone with first-pitch fastballs than they were a decade ago, or a half-decade ago. They're attacking right away, even with the pitch they know batters are expecting. The message is pretty clear: batters are being too passive.

Sliders, curves, and changeups each have more of the zone when thrown on the first pitch than they did several years ago, too, though the effect is less pronounced. Pitchers have seen the numbers; they know batters are doing better on the first pitch itself. They still feel safe throwing more and better strikes than ever before, figuring they'll come out ahead as long as they keep getting ahead to open each battle.

The Moneyball revolution brought an increased league-wide focus on OBP, which resulted in a de facto mandate to take a more patient tack at the plate. It worked very well for a while, as batters with poor plate discipline were compelled to either adjust or be expelled from the league, and pitchers with poor control were slowly weeded out.

However, concurrent with that revolution, and spurred by it in some ways, was the evolution of the pitching paradigm that now dominates the game. As batters ratcheted up their focus on inflating pitch counts and working walks, pitchers honed theirs on throwing strikes and missing bats. The league's understanding of what makes a good pitcher improved at least as much, from the mid-1990s through the mid-2000s, as its understanding of what makes a good hitter. As amphetamines and other performance-enhancing drugs were phased mostly out of the game, and as PITCHf/x broke onto the scene, individuals and teams learned how to exploit the evolved approaches of even the smartest hitters.

The ability to avoid making outs is still the most valuable one in baseball, but the magnitude of its eclipse of slugging is smaller than ever. To a greater extent than power, on-base skills derive their value from chaining—from the on-base skill levels of the players on either side of a given individual. Eleven years ago, when the housing crisis hit, people learned the hard way that the value of their homes depended a good deal on the values of their neighbors' homes. The same wasn't true, though, of their cars. So it is now, with OBP and SLG.

The global OBP in 2018 was .318. The only seasons since the Dead Ball Era in which the league got on base at a worse clip were 2013-2015, 1988, 1971-1972, and 1963-1968. This is all happening despite the aforementioned evolution of the science of hitting. It's happening despite a shift in approach and focus, one that would steer OBP ever higher, if only it were working.

Instead, it's sitting at a low ebb, and while it does so, even guys who get on base often are a little less helpful than they were 10 years ago—or 20, or 40, or 60, or 70, or 80, or 90. They're less helpful, that is, because unless there happen to be three or four other guys in the lineup who get on just as regularly, their contribution is merely to forestall the inevitable. Runs happen, increasingly, when a sudden bang happens, and that means attacking early in the count—because pitchers are sure as hell doing that.

In a league making contact on barely 75 percent of its swings, and a league in which an increasing number of pitchers can throw multiple off-speed pitches for strikes in any count, the only way to consistently generate offense is going to be aggressive. This isn't necessarily true for individuals, like Mookie Betts and Jose Ramirez, who make a lot of contact and have excellent plate discipline, and whose power comes from such natural quickness in a short stroke. Most players have to make tradeoffs, though, whether it be lowering their contact rate or raising their chase rate, in order to consistently make the quality of contact necessary to survive in today's game.

Highest %	Lowest %
Javier Baez – 48.3	Joe Mauer – 4.6
Freddie Freeman – 47.1	Mookie Betts – 9.7
Ozzie Albies – 46.3	Brett Gardner – 10.7
Jose Altuve – 44.2	Jose Ramirez – 12.0
Nick Castellanos – 44.1	Jason Kipnis – 13.8
Joey Gallo – 42.3	Jesus Aguilar – 14.5
Corey Dickerson – 40.9	Xander Bogaerts – 15.8
Salvador Perez – 40.8	Brian Dozier – 16.3
Eddie Rosario – 40.7	Mike Trout – 17.6
Nick Ahmed – 40.4	Yasmani Grandal – 17.6

Top 10 and Bottom 10 Hitters, First-Pitch Swing Rate (2018)

The question isn't which of these lists one prefers, but what they each convey, qualitatively, about the cat-and-mouse game of early-count hitting. Those top five on the left, especially, drive home the fact that for most players, getting aggressive early in the count is now key to keeping strikeout rate down and hitting for power.

For now, the message is: pitchers are coming right after batters with the nastiest stuff they've ever had. Batters had better stop giving away strike one and force hurlers to adjust, or the global OBP crisis is only going to get worse. ■

—Matthew Trueblood is an author of Baseball Prospectus.

A Hymn for the Index Stat

Patrick Dubuque

We survived without computers. I know this, because I remember the day when my dad hooked up his brand-new Atari 400 computer to the back of our 12-inch Magnavox television, and the perfect blue of the memo pad lit up for the first time. I was born just on the edge of that transitional generation, of learning cursive and balancing checkbooks and just doing math all the time, constant manual arithmetic.

It still amazes me. We learned how to sail ships without computers. We learned how to do calculus. We built towers that didn't fall down, most of the time. We engineered catapults to knock them down anyway. We built a robust system of philosophy called "utilitarianism," founded on the principle that the good of an action is evaluated by summing the effects of that action, which is the kind of formula that would make the world's mainframes crash. The whole foundation of statistics as a field is "here's math you could easily do but would die of old age first."

The fact of the matter is that there is too much math in the world to do. There are too many things changing, and too many things too small to notice, for us to handle. At some point, they become too much for the computers to handle as well, which is why we have chaos theory and undetectable earthquakes, but it's not an even fight. At some point, we fall back on intuition, and given how under-equipped we are, we're forced to bestow that intuition with some sort of supernatural superiority, the "gut feeling," that we can't prove because we can only intuit that our intuition is better.

We're all lousy at intuition, and wonderful at lying to ourselves about it. The honest truth is that computers are far better at intuition than we are, because in order to know what feels "off" you have to know what's "on." In order to do that you have to constantly reassess the average of everything, then re-rank your own experience against it.

Test your own, by comparing these three anonymous lines:

Player	G	HR	AVG	OBP	SLG
Player A	156	38	.259	.342	.535
Player B	154	38	.280	.348	.527
Player C	158	38	.266	.343	.509

These all seem like pretty similar players, right? The second one a touch more batted-ball dependent, the third a little less strong, but all pretty good hitters. And you'd be right, about the latter. Not the former.

Here's the breakdown:

- Player A: 1991 Howard Johnson, 141 DRC+
- Player B: 1996 Dean Palmer, 121 DRC+
- Player C: 2018 Giancarlo Stanton, 114 DRC+

Baseball is fortunate to have escaped the seismic shifts of so many other sports, where the talents and performances of other eras are nearly unrecognizable. (And not just other sports: try to explain the greatness of the movie Duck Soup without adjusting for era.) But they're still there, and they're nearly impossible to account for manually, without having to resort to sweeping generalizations like "steroid era" or juiced-ball era" to throw out entire swathes of production.

This is all to say that we should celebrate the index stat, that simple 100-based scale with such a humble aim: just to give context. It's hard to imagine how we lived without them for so long. Sabermetricians have always tried to make their stats look like other stats: True Average mapped to batting average, FIP molded to look like and compare to ERA. It's easy to understand the motivation—these statistics carry an emotional value in them that is hard to resist, as with the .300 hitter and the 2.00 ERA—but even they fall prey to the same loss of scale as their unadjusted counterparts. If a .300 average means different things in different years, does that hold true for a .300 True Average?

Instead, 100 doesn't say anything, except above average or below. And it does it instantly, for every season in every run environment for any statistic we want it to. We should have more index stats: K%+, so we can stop comparing Mike Clevinger's career 9.46 K/9 to Nolan Ryan's 9.55. HBP%+, so we can note that Ron Hunt was getting plunked when nobody else was getting plunked, as opposed to that imitator Brandon Guyer. Some might note how stale these references are and accuse league-adjustment as a backward-looking drive, and this is true. But we're always looking backward, always comparing the new with the expectations already set. The index stat just forces us to be honest.

There's always resistance to a new statistic, especially one so outwardly simple and so internally complex. We tend to stick with what we know, even in the case of formulas that are supposed to tell us what we know. But if your resistance is that it seems too complicated, too counterintuitive, too "black boxy," I encourage you to consider why you feel that way. Because the real world is infinitely more complicated than baseball, where all the pitches go in one basic direction and the baserunners are only allowed to travel in four directions. Baseball statistics based on mixed methodology are almost impossibly intricate. So are skyscrapers and automobiles. That's why we have computers—to take the guesswork out of them.

—Patrick Dubuque is an author of Baseball Prospectus.

Index of Names

Alcantara, Sergio 96

Alcantara, Victor 50

Alexander, Tyler 97

Azocar, Jose 96

Baez, Sandy 52

Beckham, Gordon 96

Boyd, Matt 54

Burrows, Beau 90, 102

Cabrera, Miguel 20

Cameron, Daz 83, 101

Candelario, Jeimer 22

Carpenter, Ryan 97

Castellanos, Nick 24

Castro, Willi 96, 106

Clemens, Kody 96, 107

Coleman, Louis 56

Deatherage, Brock 96

Dixon, Brandon 26

Faedo, Alex 91, 103

Farmer, Buck 58

Fernandez, Jose 97

Fulmer, Michael 60

Funkhouser, Kyle 92, 104

Goodrum, Niko 28

Greene, Shane 62

Greiner, Grayson 30

Guzman, Carlos 105

Hall, Matt 97

Hardy, Blaine 64

Harrison, Josh 32

Hernandez, Wilkel 107

Hicks, John 34

Hill, Derek 84

Houston, Zac 97

Jimenez, Eduardo 97

Jimenez, Joe 66

Jones, JaCoby 36

Kozma, Pete 96

Liniak, Kingston 96

Lugo, Dawel 38

Mahtook, Mikie 40

Manning, Matt 93, 100

Meadows, Parker 85, 105

Mercer, Jordy 42

Mize, Casey 94, 99

Moore, Matt 68

Norris, Daniel 71

Paredes, Eduardo 97

Paredes, Isaac 86, 100

Perez, Franklin 95, 102

Perez, Wenceel 87, 106

Peterson, Dustin 88

Reininger, Zac 97

Reyes, Victor 44

Rivera, Reynaldo 96

Robson, Jake 96

Rodriguez, Elvin 106

Rodriguez, Ronny 46

Rogers, Jake 89, 103

Ross, Tyson 73

Shore, Logan 97

Skubal, Tarik 107

Detroit Tigers 2019

Soto, Gregory 97
Stewart, Christin 48, 105
Stumpf, Daniel 75
Turnbull, Spencer 77

VerHagen, Drew 79
Wilson, Bobby 96
Zimmermann, Jordan 81

Ballpark diagrams for Baseball Prospectus are created by THIRTY81Project, a design concept offering original ballpark artwork, including the new 'Ballparks of 2019' 11 x 17 color print.

Visit **www.thirty81project.com** for full details.

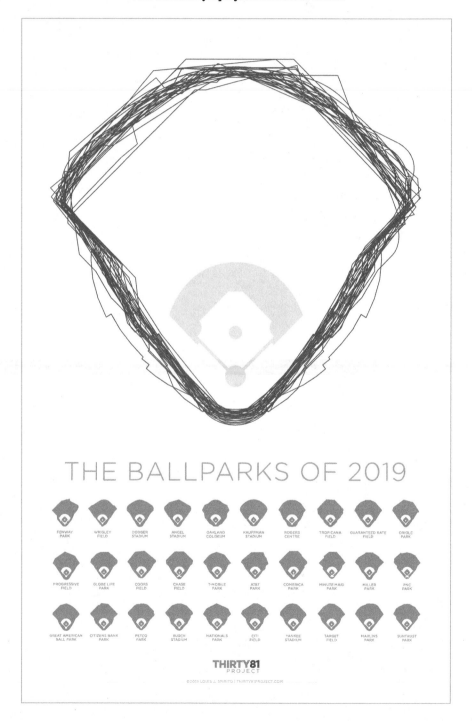